Inspired

Publisher
BIS Publishers
Herengracht 370-372
1016 CH Amsterdam
P.O. Box 323
1000 AH Amsterdam
The Netherlands
T +31 (0)20 5247560
F +31 (0)20 5247557
bis@bispublishers.nl
www.bispublishers.nl

Concept, design, photography
Dorte Nielsen and Kiki Hartmann
www.inspiredbook.com

Artwork
Frank Boon

ISBN 90-6369-110-6

Printed in Singapore.

Inspired

How creative people think, work and find inspiration

Dorte Nielsen   Kiki Hartmann

Contents

Exploring the secrets of the creative thinker

This is a book about the creative process.
The journey that starts with a blank sheet of paper and an open mind.

We've both been lucky enough to be able to work with many creative people. People, seemingly able to create wonderful, original ideas out of nothing. What has always fascinated us, is where these ideas come from. Maybe they are lurking amongst the piles of sketches, notebooks and obscure magazines that often clutter a creative thinker's desk. Maybe it's something to do with the unusual objects they surround themselves with.

Armed with a digital camera, a tape recorder and a handbag full of pens and paper, we set off around Europe to find out. We interviewed creative thinkers from a wide variety of disciplines. We asked them how and where they get their best ideas, what they surround themselves with and if they follow any kind of formula in the creative process.

They showed us their sketchbooks, notepads and bottom drawers.
They told us how they motivate themselves, what makes them tick and what gets their creative juices going.

It has been a truly fascinating experience for us. We hope you will enjoy, as we did, the heaps of stories and images we wound up collecting.
We also hope this book leaves you feeling the same way we do: Inspired.

Kiki and Dorte

Marksteen Adamson

Creative Director and Founder of
Arthur Steen Adamson
Maidenhead, UK

During his fifteen-year career,
Marksteen has built a reputation
as an inspiring creative strategist.
He has written numerous articles
on the subject of corporate and
brand identity. As a member of the
Interbrand Group's Global Steering
Committee, Marksteen played a
significant role in elevating the level
of creativity across the worldwide
organisation. Before leaving his
position as global creative director,
he created and directed numerous
identity programmes for which he
has collected several awards. In
2002, he set up his own agency,
where he continues to create
distinctive work, most notably for
St. Kea, and more recently the
British Library's 26th international
exhibition, for which he created the
world's largest edible poster.

Inspiration

Most things inspire me. People I meet and things I see.
People who live in the street. I love going into toy and
gadget shops to see the latest ideas. I love ephemeral
stuff too. Things that most people throw away; newspapers, wrappers, toys from fast food joints. I very rarely
get inspired by design books. I find them boring and
derivative variations on the same themes.
I love reading books and articles about new thinking and
social issues that are not related to our industry. Motor-
bikes inspire me. Trash movie cultures like Batman,
Spiderman and Star Wars, and movies in general
(except Hollywood happy shit). Music is a big part of
my inspiration. I compose and play. I'm inspired by the
people I work with, my kids and my mother.
And last but not least, God. All you need to do is look
around at creation and it humbles you. It is the ultimate
inspiration. The bush in Tanzania, my Maglite, thermos,
sleeping bag, tent and sunset. It's all you need.

Working environment

I don't think that you can manufacture an environment
for generating ideas. You either have great ideas or you
don't. If you want to have real new ideas you need to get
out. Go and see a great film, go to a fantastic restaurant,
fly to Paris, go on safari, hang out with the homeless,
get drunk, eat lots of chocolate, listen to your friends,
have a bath, drive nowhere for a whole night. You might
just think of something original. Most importantly, don't
try to have an idea. Just BE and it will come to you.

Working process

I start out by changing the brief. Most briefs are based
on what people think they want rather than what they
actually need. I like to work out what the real objective
is and then finding a bigger idea that can deliver the
objective in a way that sells itself rather than having to
be sold. My best ideas can come at any time. I can have
them live in meetings or when I'm on my way somewhere. But the best time is just before I go to sleep.
I always have a note book next to my bed and I get up
several times during the night to jot things down if I'm
on a roll. To get into the right frame of mind, I might get
my little notebook out, sit in front of the telly and
channel hop. I like watching all the ads. They relax me
more than the programmes. Drink some wine or beer,
but not too much, and then if I'm still stuck, I go through
my magazine collection. A long drive to nowhere is also
very good. Don't have a destination – just drive and
drive and drive. Eventually you will drive into your idea.
The best form of transport is a fast motorbike.

Motivation

Global Brand Domination.

Reading

I read Bill Bryson, Malcolm Gladwell, Nick Hornby,
The Week, National Geographic, Allan Carr, *The Sun,
The Economist, The Telegraph, The Mirror, The Bible.*

Most inspiring person

My mum.

"I had a very surreal experience when I was working as executive creative director on a well-known mobile phone account. I turned up to one of their meetings and came into the room to discover toys and random gadgets in the middle of a round table. It was a 'brain storm' organised by the internal 'innovations' department. The man leading the session was wearing a black jumper tucked into his tight black chinos halfway up his waist and on the jumper he had Velcro that allowed him to stick words and letters like a modular alphabet where you could change the words depending on your mood. Imagine a black walking fridge. On this special day he had decided to spell out 'Imagination' on his jumper. He then proceeded to ask us to free our minds and start the creative process. He asked all of us what our fears were and I was last. My answer was very simple. I replied "YOU". He was an experienced corporate diplomat and I don't think he understood what I meant. At the end of the session – just like all the other sessions he had conducted in the past – there were no real ideas and everyone left feeling 'emotionally paedophiled'."

BOOK NO. 5

elastic is put behind nose by cutting top half of nose. This will hold book together

Embosed nose

① ② ③

SCULPTURE OF CAT

TAIL

HAPPY DOG

niceday fox paper

Fax paper

Chicken pox
chicken pox

cho chicken fax.

puppy fox.

sickday

niceday fax p

niceday fax p

niceday

DON'T KNOW

Glaz hou

MAUBE

transparent
re-enforcement
washers

niceday
transparent
re enforcement
washers

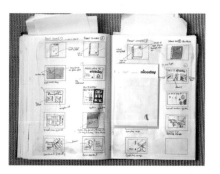

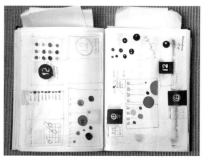

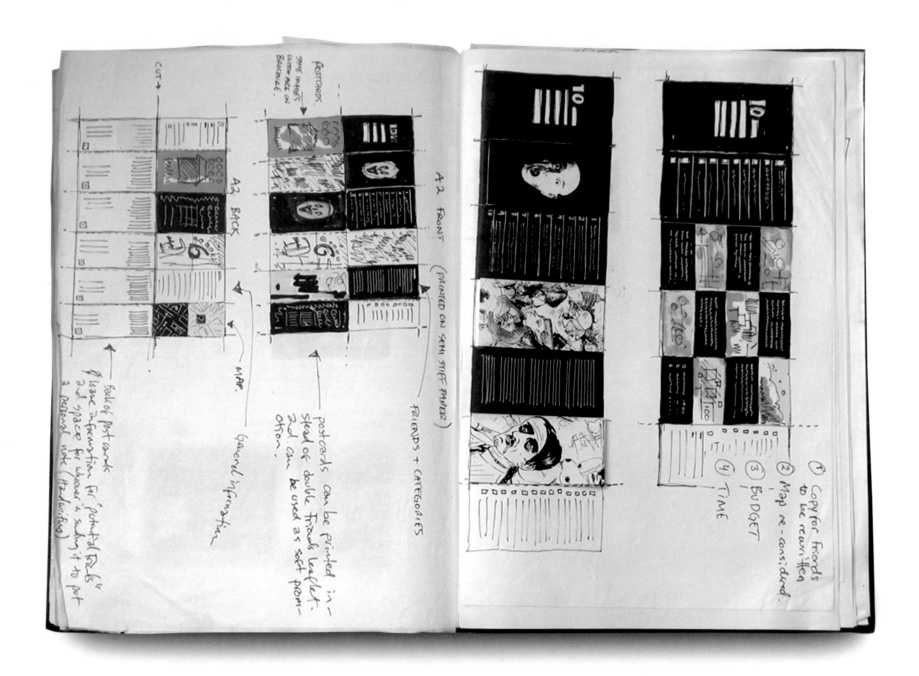

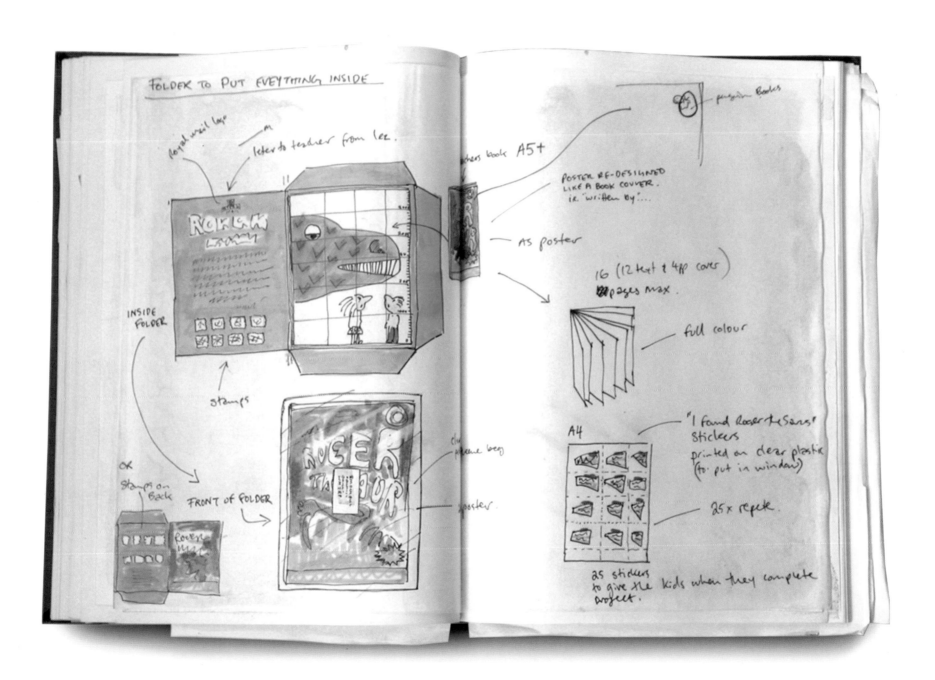

Andy Altmann

Graphic Designer, Co-Founder and
Partner of Why Not Associates
London

After earning a BA Hons in graphic
design from Saint Martins School
of Art, London and an MA (RCA)
from the Royal College of Art,
London, Andy co-founded
Why Not Associates in 1987 with
fellow partner David Ellis and
former partner Howard Greenhalgh.
Why Not Associates is a multi-
disciplinary design studio, renowned
for creating highly innovative and
varied work. As a partner, Andy has
worked for the past 17 years on
many major projects spanning a
wide range of media. He has also
lectured worldwide on the company's work, in such countries as
Australia, America, Africa and Japan.

Inspiration

I get inspiration from anything and everything. It could
be from a book, my child or anything with type – even
bad type. I collect stuff. Lots of stuff.
I keep scrapbooks, sketchbooks and paper clippings.
At the Royal College, we had to make scrapbooks, but
because I couldn't draw very well I had to stick stuff
down. I don't bother with them as much now. I use my
Mac instead as a way of sketching.

Working environment

I like a calm environment, like this office. I like being
surrounded by lots of things. I guess it's not so obvious
here but the old one was much messier. Here, things are
in cupboards, hidden away. But we know where they are
if we need them.

Working process

There's no formula as to how I get my best ideas.
Normally my first idea is best. I try to go away and think
of other things, but I keep coming back to the first one,
thinking I'm not going to better that idea.
The ability to see a good idea is down to instinct and
experience. When you're a student you tend to have
400 different ideas. With experience you can narrow it
down faster. What it could be, and what it should be.
I think one of our strengths is the ability to see a good
idea. If I get stuck, or go round and round in circles,
I try to look at things in a different context.

Reading

I only read books when I'm on holiday, and then I
read lots. I prefer historical novels, like *Dan Leno and
the Limehouse Golem* by Peter Ackroyd for example.

Most inspiring person

George Best. He played with great flair and imagination.
He did the unexpected and didn't follow the rules.

"I couldn't draw very well, so I had to stick stuff down"

 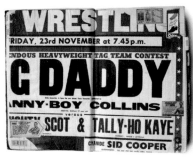  

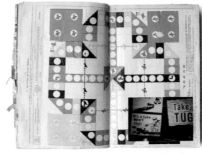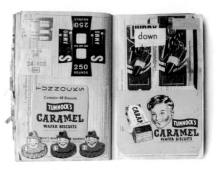

the physique of a toothpick
and the pallor of a child raised on chip butties ...

Ex-soccer star held

Holding—direct free kick

Pushing—direct free kick

"birds kept me sane," declared best

"I get inspiration from anything and everything"

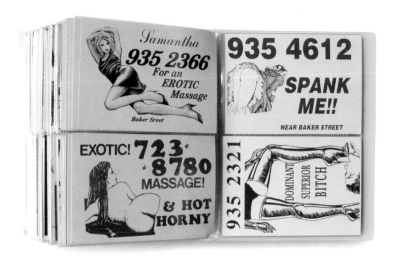

Rosie Arnold
Creative Director,
Bartle Bogle Hegarty
London

After studying at Bournemouth
College of Art, and later at Central
St. Martins, Rosie joined the
renowned London advertising
agency Bartle Bogle Hegarty where
she has enjoyed many years of
success. She has won numerous
industry awards for her work with
clients such as Lynx and Levi's.
Her awards include four Cannes
Gold Lions, a coveted D&AD
pencil and Campaign Golds.

Inspiration

I've always found inspiration in the events of ordinary
everyday life. I also love travelling – or journeys. They
don't have to be exotic, they can be everyday journeys to
and from work. It's the moments that occur while I'm
out and about that inspire me.
It's also amazing how inspiring children can be. Their
view of things can turn you upside down. Suddenly you
find yourself in a different world. A world of stories,
colouring books and magic. I get a lot of ideas from the
stuff I do with my own children.
Jokes are another great source of inspiration. A really
good joke forces you to look at things differently. But it's
not just what you say. It's how you tell them. I also draw
a lot of inspiration from photography.

Working environment

I collect art and paintings. I also collect things like little
wooden boxes. I have scrapbooks full of cuttings and
ideas. I keep clippings, photographs and boxes of magazines. I've also got boxes full of ideas and old scripts.

Working process

I approach a job with enthusiasm and work from
personal experience. I enjoy turning stories and previous
experiences into ads. I have a store of memories that
I can draw on.
I might think about how the brief or the product
relates to me, and how I feel about it and that might

just create a new idea. Misreading something can also
spark great ideas. I usually get my best ideas when
I stop thinking about a particular project or problem.
I find ideas come to me when I go to the park.
Investigation can also lead to ideas. If I get stuck,
I might find somebody to bounce ideas off, or get out
of the office and start using my eyes.

I also find change stimulating – ironic coming from me!
Same job, same house, same husband, but I do have
a terrible tendency to paint rooms, move furniture and
never ever have a routine. I never take the same route,
let alone transport to work. It's wonderful because I see
new things every time. Whether travelling by bus, tube,
bike or car.

Reading

I read fanatically. I'd rather read than watch television.
I really love classics. I can't trace any specific idea back
to a book, but reading helps me get into the head of
the consumer.

Motivation

The bank manager. I'm motivated by the need to pay
bills. To have a roof over ones head, food on the table
and Manolo Blahniks on ones feet.

Most inspiring person

John Hegarty.

Extracts from a speech Rosie
made for the Campaign
Creative Conference.

"The sights you see, the adventures
you have are food for the brain visually and verbally. To prove this point
I took out a digital camera and trav-
elled around Soho just to see what
I could find in half an hour within a
short radius.

"Handel and Jimi Hendrix. How
fantastic that they lived next door!"

"I've always loved crushed tin cans."

"At the same time I went out with
the Lynx Effect brief in mind. For
those of you unfamiliar with the
campaign, the idea is that Lynx helps
young men get the girls. Look what

I found all in that same half an hour.
Interesting how many ideas are out
there if you open your eyes."

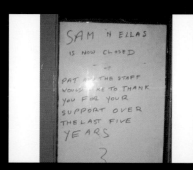

"Read it to yourself – now can you
see why they went out of business?"

"What inspires me about this
painting is the colour, its boldness,
its energy and naivety and the fact
that my children painted it, aged
four and six. It's amazing how fan-
tastically inspiring children can be."

"Jokes are a great source of inspiration. A really good joke forces you to look at things differently"

Per Arnoldi
Artist
Copenhagen

Per was born in 1941 and started exhibiting his work in galleries and museums in the late sixties. Today he is one of Denmark's foremost graphic artists. He is represented at numerous prominent international galleries including the Museum of Modern Art in New York, the Toyama Museum of Modern Art in Japan, London's Victoria and Albert Museum, the Stedelijk Museum in Amsterdam and the Israel Museum in Jerusalem. He has created posters for clients such as the Guggenheim Museum in New York, the Chicago Symphony Orchestra, the Montreux Jazz Festival and the Royal Theatre, Copenhagen. In recent years, Per has collaborated with Norman Foster and Partners, London and during his career has received a great many awards for his work both in Denmark and internationally.

Inspiration

Having ideas and creating is like the food chain; it's self-nourishing. For every job I do, I have to run through 25 different solutions or directions, 24 of which won't be used. In this way, I accumulate 24 ideas that I won't use immediately, but might offer the perfect starting point for something else at a later stage.

I'm always working. I exhibited for the first time when I was 17. I'm now 65. I've gathered lots of experience. My idea bank is full. I can draw on all the things I remember, and I enjoy turning a dead end into a new way forward.

I don't go for long walks along the beach for inspiration. Instead I have 'nature experiences' in my studio. I find the splashes and stains on the floor very inspiring. I think my paint rag is interesting. Sometimes I think it's even better than my painting.

Working environment

Space, lots of space. I need it to work in.

All I collect is knowledge and anecdotes. I am a story-teller and collector, a raconteur, and I have quite a few African pieces for the same reason: They are a story condensed in clear form. I like folk art and simple objects.

Working process

I have this feeling that all ideas already exist somewhere. I make myself receptive to them by being naïve, by emptying my head completely. I sit down, make coffee or look at a painting. I try to feel the ideas in the back of my head and see how they're doing.

You can't force them to appear, and you cannot make them disappear either! I might stand and watch paint dry, then leave again, or do something practical. Then I change my identity. I try to become the story I am going to tell. A good impersonator starts by 'becoming' who he is going to impersonate. The ideas start to appear when I'm in my receptive mode. It's a state of mind. Or rather, a state of mindlessness.

When working in London, Japan or anywhere else in the world (I travel some 190 days a year) I always eat alone, at the same restaurant, at the same table. I sit with a pad and write. I create lists all the time, and I doodle. Going to the same place time after time gives me the peace I need to work.

Reading

I don't read enough. I enjoy looking at photography books in my spare time. I find some photographers particularly interesting, such as Lartigue, who took his first picture when he was five. He considered himself a professional painter, but ended up being the world's best amateur photographer... it's a strange story that puzzles me endlessly.

Motivation

What makes me get up every morning and paint a blue square? I keep thinking that maybe the next one will be the best one ever. I hope that one day I will succeed.

Most inspiring person

Picasso. He's a great inspiration.
Orson Welles, who never gave up.

"Sometimes I think my paint rag is even better than my painting"

PER ARNOLDI'S COMBINED STUDIO
AND HOME IN CENTRAL COPENHAGEN.

"I need lots
of space
to work in"

Simon Bang
Storyboard Artist
Copenhagen

Simon was born in 1960 and studied at Skolen for Brugskunst (now Danmark's Designskole). As well as working and teaching as a commercial storyboard artist, his diverse career has encompassed books, exhibitions, record sleeves, posters, graphic logos and film titles. He has also created production sketches and storyboards for many famous films such as *Pelle the Conqueror, Smilla's Sense of Snow, Les Miserables, Heart of Light, Beyond, Old Men in New Cars, Someone Like Hodder* and the television series *Taxa* and *Unit 1.*

Inspiration

Inspiration isn't something that suddenly comes to you. The route to good work is working hard. I think the most inspiring thing is when your desk is tidy, your finances are in order, and you have a white sheet of paper in front of you.

It's different when your creativity needs recharging. I go for walks to experience and observe. I look at people, the streets and the light. I might visit a bookshop, go to the cinema or see an exhibition. I like observing people. I watch the way a man puts on his hat and think: "What kind of a life has that man had?".

I collect a lot. I'm terrible. I collect irons in their packaging, cigarette cartons with cigarettes in them, metal boxes, posters, drawings, prints, letters, signs, ceramics, glass, books and curiosities.

Working environment

I surround myself with things I care for and objects I find either beautiful or visually interesting.

Working process

Storyboarding is what I primarily do. I'm classically trained and was taught to observe. When working on films, I usually sit and work with the director, as I'm good at listening and sketch very fast.

I find conversation very inspiring. Ideas are created by dialogue, comparisons, metaphors, funny or serious observations, etc. I ask questions, I try to be analytical, and see the task from all possible angles. I prepare myself for a meeting by giving myself time to clear my head. I need peace and quiet for about an hour beforehand. I put on a clean shirt. I might spend the time cycling there because it is a good way of getting into the right frame of mind. It gives you the clear and open mind of a child.

When working on my own, I make a conscious effort to avoid repeating the same working patterns. I'm constantly trying to develop the way I think and work. I never get stuck. If things don't happen during the process, I go back to the beginning and start from scratch again.

Motivation

For me, work is a calling. I think days that are wasted are dreadful.

Reading

I read a lot of fiction and non-fiction. I enjoy books about art and film and how they are created. I subscribe to three different newspapers and also read news from CNN and the BBC, plus a lot of other stuff on the web. I read film and graphic design magazines, I browse through hundreds of books and buy a lot for reference.

Most inspiring person

Stanley Kubrik. He's a fantastic example of how to stay in control of your work.

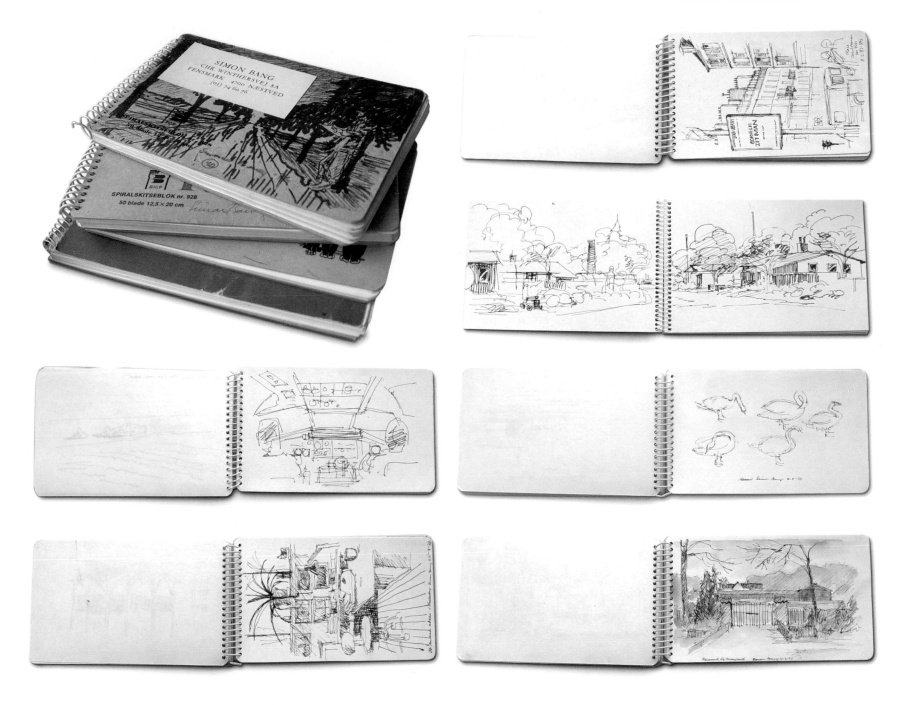

"I think the most inspiring thing is when your desk is tidy, your finances are in order and you have a white sheet of paper in front of you"

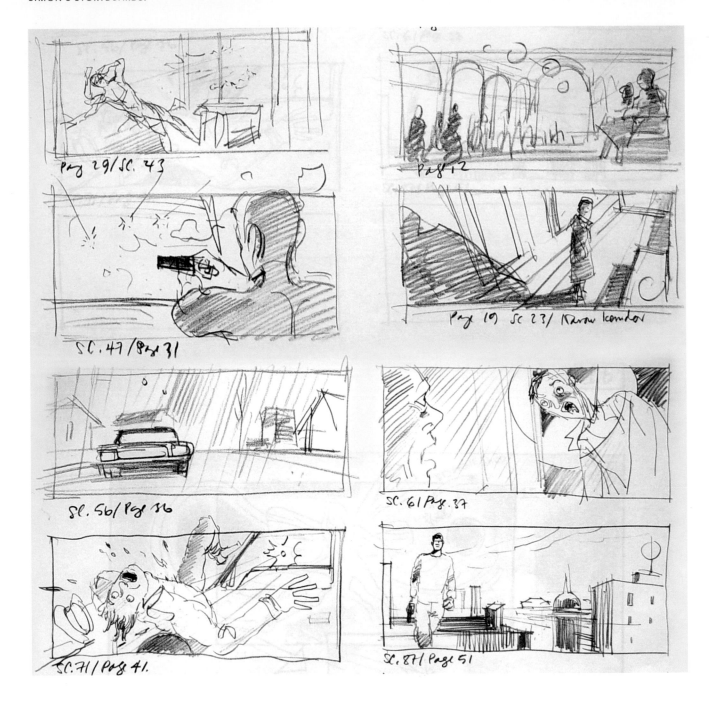

Pag 29/SC. 43

SC. 47/Pag 31

SC. 56/Pag 36

SC. 71/Pag 41.

Pag 12

Pag 19/ SC 23/ Kerow kondor

SC. 61 Pag. 37

SC. 87/ Pag 51

"I make a conscious effort
to avoid repeating the same
working patterns.
I'm constantly trying to develop
the way I think and work"

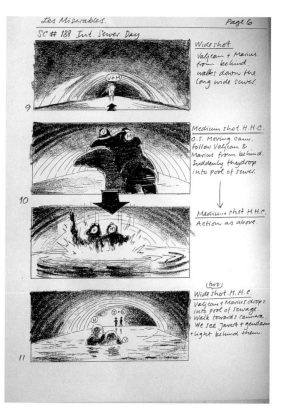

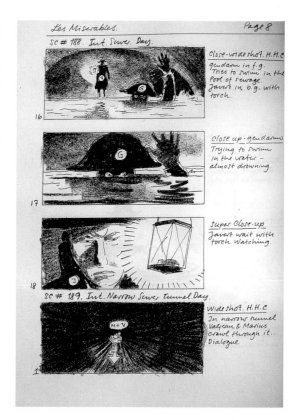

Georgie Bean
Interior Stylist and Producer,
freelance Magazine Correspondent
Amsterdam

Georgie was born in Portland,
a small coastal town outside
Melbourne, Australia. In the early
nineties, she studied interior design
in London while working at Habitat
on the King's Road. After returning
to Australia, she joined *Vogue Living*
magazine as assistant to the
Melbourne editor, before moving
over to the new magazine
Marie Claire Lifestyle as merchandise
editor. In 2000, she moved to
Amsterdam with her Dutch husband
and joined *Wallpaper** magazine
as correspondent for the Benelux
area, as well as freelancing for
other publications.

Inspiration
Travelling is a huge source of inspiration for me as
it always seems to open my mind to more ideas.
I love travelling in Europe and experiencing other
cultures, food, art and fashion. I collect lots of 'things',
particularly unique fabrics, wallpapers and magazines,
but I am not a keen collector of anything in particular.
I love to find interesting shops that offer unique things
that you do not see anywhere else. I'm quite senti-
mental and have a collection of shells and pebbles from
various beaches around the world that remind me of
my childhood years spent beachcombing. The most
important things to me are family and friends. If you are
lucky enough to have both, then inspiration will come.

Working environment
I have created my own resourceful home office, where
I can sit down and go through a whole variety of
magazines and books for inspiration, as well as my
files full of the latest catalogues, brochures, tear sheets
and photographs. My laptop is in constant use and a
thesaurus is always close by. Things I've collected over
time always have relevance at some point later on.
I use Polaroid books and scrapbooks that are more like
recollections of memories, and I like to use sketchbooks
as my notebooks.

Working process
Each job is different, so I rarely use the same approach
twice. Often my work comes together as a collective

project, usually involving a photographer and myself,
but also an editor and an art director of a magazine.
I love my work, as each job is different and I meet great
creative and interesting people, as well as working with
beautiful objects and designs.
Being freelance makes you appreciate when you have
work, as there is no guarantee when the next job will be.

I get my best ideas when I'm on the move. I love that
travel time in a plane or train when I can stare out of
the window and daydream.

Whenever I get stuck, I try to leave the project for a
while and hope the ideas will come. If I have time,
I might go shopping or to a gallery, or just take a walk
to clear my head.

Motivation
Seeing my work published is a great feeling.

Reading
I read newspapers because their design sections are
always more up to the minute than magazines, but I
also read foreign, interior, lifestyle and niche magazines.

Most inspiring person
There is not one person. However, a quality I really
admire in people is initiative. People who are not afraid
to give something a go, carry things through, and
believe in what they're doing.

"I love these vintage wallpapers, found in an amazing old shop in Ghent, Belgium"

"Things I've collected over time always have relevance at some point later on"

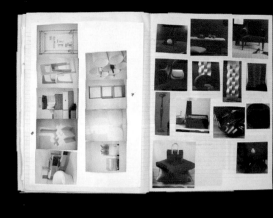

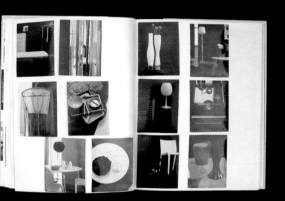

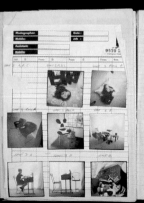

Andy Bird

Creative Partner, Soul Advertising
London

Andy started his career in 1988
at McCann Erickson working as a
typographer. He left in 1993 to join
Butterfield Day Devito Hockney,
where he became head of design.
Another move saw Andy join
Bartle Bogle Hegarty, where he
spent six years as an art director/
designer and eventually became
head of art. Here, he was
responsible for the visual output
of the agency and won awards
spanning a wide range of clients.
In 2000, Andy started up Soul
Advertising as a founding partner.

Inspiration

I'm inspired by real life and by people, either people I
know or people I meet. I'm inspired by observations.
I used to do scrapbooks and notebooks. Now I only
doodle but I don't keep the doodles.
And I collect Adidas trainers. I have about 250 pairs.

Working environment

I think it's important not to be precious about your
own space. At Soul we all sit in one open space. Mixed
creatives, with no barriers between departments. It's
easier to generate ideas when there's collaboration
between people. So I don't surround myself with many
personal things. All I've got on my desk is my Mac.

Working process

I take each job as it comes. You have to have a different
outlook for each client and I always start by doodling.
It's important to start by hand, so I never go to the
computer first.
I get my best ideas when I take my time and
concentrate. Actually, I think as well when I'm away
from my desk as when I'm at it. You should always

be thinking and noticing stuff. I find you have to spend
time on great design and art direction.

I always try to establish a look as well as an idea. I think
keeping things simple is the most important thing.
A good idea can be spoilt by bad art direction. Over-
complicated design can sometimes get in the way of
the message.

If I get stuck, I talk to other people. Most of the time
that's my creative partner, Bruce.

Reading

I read *Eye magazine*, *Creative Review*,
www.swinemagazine.co.uk and *Viz*.

Most inspiring person

Alan Shearer.

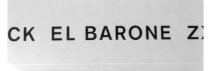

"Every member of staff was allowed one word to put on the wall. It had to be a word that was close to their 'soul' to tie in with our name"

GAZELLE   MARATHON 'TR'   GRAND SLAM   VOLLEYBALL   TOBACCO

ZX-8000   MANCHESTER   SPEZIAL   JEANS   SL 7

WIMBLEDON   ADIRUNNER   ZX-500   KOPEN

ACHILLE

INDOOR SUPER

MARATHON

PARIS MARATHON

ZX-500

SL 72

"Adidas 1970–1989.
Loads of smelly old shoes"

Henrik Birkvig
Typographer, The Graphic Arts
Institute of Denmark
Copenhagen

Henrik was born in 1955. He studied
film at Copenhagen University
during the seventies before
continuing his education at The
Graphic Arts Institute and graduating in 1982 as a graphic designer.
He later returned as a member of
the faculty and has held various
head-of-department positions since
the early nineties. Henrik has taught
a variety of subjects, but recently
decided to focus on typography and
calligraphy. He is the author of
numerous books and articles on
graphic design and communication,
and freelances as well as lectures as
a graphic designer and consultant.

Inspiration
I'm inspired by everyday life.

Working environment
I surround myself with books, computers and lots of
notes. I collect doodles, rubbings and publications
about type and calligraphy.

Working process
I approach a job by starting with the boring stuff:
analysis, setting up a document with formats etc. I close
the door, take my time and browse through books and
magazines.

I get my best ideas in the loo, in the shower, just before
sleeping, driving the car, watching television or something complete different that is entirely unconnected to
a given problem.

If I get stuck, I start with all the 'classic' techniques:
mind mapping, or those presented in *Idea Index* or
Bob Gill's books.

I keep idea banks. I doodle and do thumbnails. I make
electronic 'sketches' by experimenting and generating
ideas without paper, using the computer to play around
with different possibilities.

Motivation
Breaking new ground. Doing something I've never
tried before, like experimenting with a new typeface or
layout idea.

Reading
I mainly read literature about design and design history.
Books such as *Tart Cards, Surprise Me, Schriftanalysen*
and *Radical graphics*. Magazines such as: *Eye magazine,
Page, CAP & Design, Typographische Monatsblätter, Emigré
magazine*, and *Dot dot dot*.

Most inspiring person
Oswald B. Cooper, designer of the famous typeface
Cooper Black. The use of this typeface often represents
a non-pretentious attitude to the design profession.

"When I'm in a boring conference or meeting, the right side of my brain wanders off"

BQCe
DEF
Profeten
PROFETEN
EVALUERING
wash
CROCE
RSV
ACD
acde
ABC
BUZZ
RS

CONTROL VALVE

AMETEK

PLYMOUTH PLASTICS

SHEBOYGAN, WIS.

"Visual research plays
an important role in the
creative game. Everywhere,
locations can become
a graphic souvenir in
the form of a rubbing"

Dick Bruna
Illustrator and Writer
The Netherlands

Born in 1927 into a family of
publishers in Utrecht, Dick started
his career as a designer and
illustrator by creating over two
thousand book covers and posters
for the 'Zwarte Beertjes' series.
However, it was a little white
bunny named Miffy that made
Dick one of the most famous
creators of picture books in the
world. He has written and
illustrated over 110 books, 27 of
which are Miffy titles. His books
have been translated into over
40 languages and have sold
nearly 85 million copies and won
numerous awards worldwide.

Inspiration
I'm inspired by very simple things. It can be a shape,
a nice red door or a blue window. I collect objects that
I like for their shape or colour.
I also collect the presents that I get from children all
over the world. I have a whole bookcase full of them.

Working environment
This studio is the perfect environment for generating
ideas. I don't surround myself with much. I'm always
cleaning up and putting things away. I'm probably
influenced by De Stijl.

Working process
I normally have a very clear idea of what I want to do
straight away. Usually the first idea I get is the best.
When I have a story in my head, I try to divide it into
twelve drawings. I sketch first and then do the final
illustration with a brush and paint.
Sometimes it can take two to three months to do twelve
drawings. I'm a perfectionist, but I never work with a
computer. When I'm working on a book, I hide it away
until it's almost ready, then I show it to my wife, who is
my best critic.

I don't get stuck, I always have enough ideas. In fact,
I seem to have more ideas the older I get. I'm always
thinking of new stories. Even when I'm on holiday I
sketch and write. It's just how I am.

I see myself more as a graphic designer than an artist
and I've designed quite a lot of book covers in my life.
The 'Zwarte Beertjes' book covers and posters became
so recognisable at one point, that I could design them
entirely without text and people still recognised them.
I'm also proud of the fact that I have inspired a lot of
children to create their own nijntje stories and drawings.

Reading
I read biographies about colleagues, musicians, writers,
and especially about French painters.

Motivation
This is my life. I couldn't do anything else. I could retire
now, but this is my hobby and what I like doing best,
so I just go on.

Most inspiring person
Henri Matisse.

"I often get inspiration from very simple things"

"I get presents from children all over the world. They are truly inspirational and special to me and I keep them all here in my studio"

"After all these years, I still get nervous every time I sit down to draw Miffy"

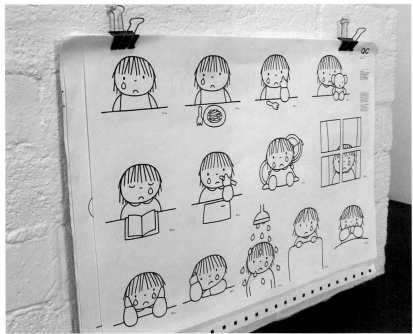

Tony Davidson and Kim Papworth

Creative Directors, Wieden+Kennedy London

Kim graduated from Epsom College of Art and Design in 1981 and started his career at Demond Advertising in London. He moved to BMP DDB Needham in 1985, where he met Tony, who had recently graduated from Manchester Polytechnic with a 1st class BA Hons in Design and Communication Media. Together they have worked at several of London's most prestigious advertising agencies, creating memorable and award-winning work for Volkswagen, Courage, Cadbury's, Heinz, Adidas, Hyundai, The Guardian, The BBC, Levi's, Audi, One2One, Murphy's Stout and Lynx. In 2000, they joined Wieden+Kennedy as joint creative directors and have continued their success, winning awards for work for Honda, Nike and others.

Inspiration

Everyone should have a digital camera. Inspiration is all around you. We take pictures of things like broken car wing mirrors and how people have fixed them.

Collecting things stimulates the brain. It helps you think of something fresher. We see something and keep it without knowing what we'll use it for. Rather than file them all online, we keep them in scrapbooks. There's something quite nice about opening a book. We use them for reference when we work.

We are very inspired by cross-culture and happy accidents. When things get mixed up the wrong way, they become fresh.

Working environment

The building you are in and the way you lay it out will affect your working environment. We have found open plan is good, but you need areas to escape to. Often, agencies try too hard to design their building to appear creative. But it is what individuals bring in from the outside that is more interesting. You have to be surrounded by ideas and cultural inspiration.

Working process

Selling a product whilst being entertaining is a discipline. You have to learn the rules, and then learn how to break them.

In advertising, you normally work to a fixed proposition that arrives in the form of a brief on your desk. We try not to focus on one proposition too early, as brands – like people – have many facets. Strategic and creative thinking done in parallel to reach the final solution. We try not to think about advertising first.

Most inspiring person

Tony: Paul Smith.
Kim: Saul Bass.

"Inspiration is all around you"

"We take pictures of weird stuff, like broken car wing mirrors, and how people have fixed them"

"You have to be surrounded by ideas and cultural inspiration"

"Collecting things stimulates the brain. It helps you think of something fresher"

Mark Denton

Commercials Director,
Partner, Therapy Film
London

Mark started his career in the
London advertising industry in 1976,
working briefly as a paste-up artist
at Bridge Advertising before moving
on to Leo Burnett as an assistant art
director. In 1984, he joined Bartle
Bogle Hegarty, where he teamed
up with Chris Palmer and started a
career-long habit of winning awards.
1986 saw a move to Lowe Howard-
Spink, where Mark and Chris
continued their success. In 1988,
they launched their own agency,
Simons Palmer Denton Clemmow,
which established itself as the most
highly awarded agency in the UK. In
1994, Mark and Chris received the
Creative Circle President's Award
for Achievement in Advertising
subsequently, they left the agency
to develop as commercial directors.
Mark continues to write and design
for advertising and television and
has been directing solo for almost
ten years.

Inspiration

I can get inspired by anything. It could be by sitting on
the bus, seeing an interesting face, an interesting outfit
or a poster. Or by watching films, musicals or cartoons.
I'm the oldest viewer of Cartoon Network. I'm interested
in everything.

I keep scrapbooks. I use them for collecting reference
material and interesting stuff, but I also use them
for work as part of the process. I keep notebooks and
clippings and I've got filing cabinets full of ideas.

Working environment

I've got a lot of reference stuff, books, videos and films,
but I prefer to surround myself with as little as possible.
I go through phases of collecting different things. At
the moment I collect sixties board games. I don't like
clutter, so I collect them and then give them away. I have
a constant flow of stuff.

I don't like buying anything that's been made by someone else. I prefer designing everything myself.

I think the best environment for generating ideas is on
the tube on my way to work. It's a place where there's
absolutely nothing to do. And that's the best time to
have ideas. Or on the bus. Yes, it doesn't get much
better than the bus. I probably get more ideas on the
bus than I do sitting here.

Working process

The job dictates the approach. I surround myself with
as much reference material as I can and then I try to
absorb as much as possible. I tend to do extra research,
either into how the target audience thinks, or into the
subject. I try to get to know everything there is to know
about something. I love work. I can't stop having ideas.
Even at home, I sit with a pad next to me. I sketch and
scribble. Ideas appear as if by magic. They just fall out of
the end of the pencil.

I believe you're either born with it or not. You can't learn
to have ideas. You can learn to discipline yourself to get
the most out of your talent, and you can enhance what
you've got, but either you've got it or you haven't.

It does get tough once in a while, but I don't get stuck
for ideas. I can always come up with something. Some
people have lots of excuses for not doing any work. Even
at college there were people who'd complain that they
couldn't produce anything because they didn't have the
right equipment. I believe that, if you're any good, you
can come up with something great with a piece of paper
and a burnt stick.

Motivation

I'm nearly 47, but I still work at weekends and on
holidays. It's in my blood. It's not like work, it's fun. I'm
being paid for doing my hobby. My biggest frustration is
not having enough hours in the day for what I want to do.

Reading

I read Sunday papers, mainly headlines and paragraphs.
I look at magazines. I find films, TV and the net stimulating. But there's too much. I haven't got enough time
to read.

Most inspiring person

Right now it's Malcolm Venville.

"I got the inspiration for doing what I'm doing today as a kid reading the *Eagle book of careers* – the section called *I want to be a commercial artist*"

festival → Britain (locomotive) type scooter.

'Volemobile'

SQUEEE!!

B B B B RRM
B B RR M
B B R MM

WICKER

SQUEEL + BRRRM S.F.X.
← CHAFFINCH RECORD

LOUD

organ stops.

EMERGENCY BRAKE

'Volescoota'

P H U T T

P H U T T

VOLESKATER

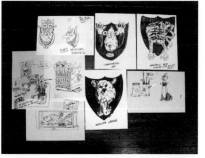

"I designed everything in my old flat myself; the wallpaper, carpets, furniture, all the clothes in the wardrobe, the stationery and even the family portraits"

Gustav Egerstedt
Art Director, Saatchi & Saatchi
Stockholm

Gustav was born in 1973 in
Stockholm, Sweden. After studying at Forsbergs advertising
school, Gustav joined Hollingworth
Mehrthora, a Stockholm advertising
agency that was re-named KING
in 2000. He has worked with
clients such as RFSU, Scan, ICA,
A non-smoking generation, Canon,
Popagandafestivalen, Tele2,
the Swedish Army and Carlsberg.
In 2005, Gustav moved to join
Saatchi & Saatchi in Stockholm.

Inspiration
Music, films, football, concerts and everyday life inspire
me. I suppose it's possible to be inspired anywhere and
by anything, as long as you're open to it.

Working environment
I collect things that I find interesting. I prefer to keep
my surroundings tidy, although they never are. It's a
constant struggle not to drown in your own stuff.

Working process
There's only one way to get a really good idea and that's
through hard work. We dissect the brief and bounce
ideas around in a group of at least three: art director,
copywriter and designer. Sometimes we put up a big
folding wall around us to create a calm corner and then
hang up all our ideas on it, good and bad.
When I relax and stop thinking too much, the ideas
usually come by themselves.
If I get stuck, I might clean my desk. It's like a re-start
and it cleans out my head too. I try to eliminate stress,
which is usually the reason why you get stuck in the first
place. Sometimes it helps to pretend that what you're
doing isn't that crucial or important (which it really
isn't anyway!).
A change of environment can also help. Leave the office,
phones and e-mail behind so that you can focus.

Motivation
I want to surprise people. I want the client to say:
"Can you really do that?"
And yes, I admit it, I want to impress my friends.

Reading
I read Douglas Coupland. I like travel and different
magazines, such as the Swedish music magazine
Sonic and comic strip *Larsson*. I get more out of those
than all the supposedly "cool" magazines. Everyone
has the same ones and they all tear out the same stuff
– not very original.

Most inspiring person
Terry Gilliam. He's a person who really has to fight for
his projects and always manages to keep his creative
integrity intact.

"I get a lot of my inspiration from music"

"There's only one way to get a really good idea and that's trough hard work"

  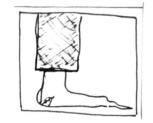 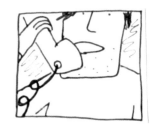  

Hörner
läten

Sovande
tehniker

Martin Galton
Creative Director,
Partner, Hooper Galton
London

Having trained as a designer,
Martin took the move to art
direction in the mid-eighties, and
joined advertising agency Bartle
Bogle Hegarty. There, he worked on
the agency's iconic Levi's account,
as well as Häagen-Dazs and many
others. In 1992, he left to join
Leagas Delaney where, as head of
art and Tim Delaney's partner, he
garnered more awards for his work
for Hyundai, Adidas and Harrods.
Pepe Jeans was voted the best campaign of all time in Europe. In 1999,
Martin co-founded Hooper Galton.

Inspiration

I once asked somebody if they liked jazz. No, they said,
listening to jazz makes me nervous. That's the sort of
reaction I like.

I like things that don't conform. Quirky things, irreverent
things, bold and daring things. Not boring or bland, who
would? If it's interesting, then I'm interested.

Mistakes are good. I really love mistakes. I like it when
you mishear things or when you've drawn something
that is not quite what you intended. I like graffiti and
scribbles, they are often unexpected, a chance.

I'm quite a restless person. My wife says I'm a creative
compulsive, which roughly translated means I'm a pain
in the arse. I get anxious and can't relax if I haven't at
least tried to create something new each day. I paint and
write a lot, poems mainly and bits of nonsense. I've got
little notebooks everywhere.

Working environment

Creative departments are often boring. Nothing much
seems to go on. All the creativity is in people's heads
but it seems odd to me that most creative people sit at
a desk hiding behind a computer.

Working process

Advertising is simple. Once you've understood the problem, you can find the right answer. All too often the real
problem isn't clear. Stick to the truth. People can spot
bullshit a mile off.

When looking at our work I ask two questions: 1. Does
our idea grab attention? If you don't do that then
everything else is irrelevant. 2. Does it say something
relevant? Bizarrely, most ads don't seem to bother,

consequently the ad isn't really of much use to anybody.
If you get those two things right, then hopefully the work
will leave an impression.

I try to find a playing field where no one else is playing.
Sometimes it takes a while but if you keep searching you
will find one eventually. It's where fresh ideas live.

When I get stuck, I sometimes borrow from one world
and apply it to another. It can get interesting when you
do that. Like applying the rules of football to the Vatican.
Why not choose a new Pope with a penalty shootout.
Sometimes I'll go to the bookshop or a music store and
stare at album covers. I like seeing how others working
in different disciplines have solved problems. Maybe I'll
go for a walk or just shut my mind off for a while. The
most tempting thing to do when problem solving, is to
look at a D&AD annual. The problem here is that all of
those ideas have been done. But it's good at reminding
you how quick and simple communication should be. I
put a lot of faith in intuition. A good gut feeling is what
separates most creative people.

Motivation

In the past it was not getting fired, but these days I just
try to have a laugh. I love what I do.

Reading

The best book I have read in years is *The curious incident
of the dog in the night-time* by Mark Haddon.

Most inspiring person

The person who has probably influenced me most is
a brilliant artist called Roy Oxlade. He taught me the
importance of risk, chance and trusting intuition.

DOES OUR IDEA DO THIS?

1. grab attention

2. say something relevant

3. leave an impression

Grab at
It's all

tention
there is

Everything I Write is Shite

Today my head is so empty
There's an echo
My brain is as dim
As the armpit
Of a gloworm
There is nothing
But a
Big
Black
Hole
Which is why I can't think of
A fucking thing today.
Just
Blank
Blank
Blankety
Blank
Blank
Blank
Blank -
But then from nowhere there is something
A brief vision
Of a naked nun
Standing in a bowl
Of engine oil –
And then it's gone.
Everything is
Blank
Blank
Blank
Blankety
Blank
Wankety

A poem for Victor

My heart
Has a tap.
And if you turn it on
You will drown
In love.

Wank
Blank
Blank
Blank.
Consequently
This poem has
No start
Middle
Or end
Just a big
Blank space.
M i n d   t h e   g a p !

Teeth

Last week
I had a tooth crowned
It's nice to have a Royal tooth

But this new Royal status
Has caused a hiatus
Amongst the
Chattering classes

It's all gone mental
In the dental
Department
As one disgruntled molar
Put it
Frankly – it's a kick in the
Teeth.

SOMETIMES MARRIAGE IS JUST
AN INVASION OF PERSONAL PRIVACY

Ed's wife was in the kitchen
thinking.
Ed was in the bath sinking
to the depths of despair.
And while she pondered
the grouting,
Ed was shouting
"Is there any hope?"
she thought he said 'soap'.
"No" she said
Now Ed is dead
His life empty and dank
he waved goodbye
and sank

I met my first wife at a party
Our eyes met across a crowded room
and she thought to herself:
One day, I'm going to divorce that man.

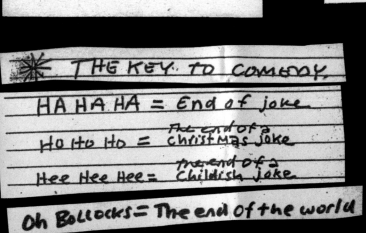

THE KEY TO COMEDY

HA HA HA = End of joke

Ho Ho Ho = The end of a christmas Joke

Hee Hee Hee = the end of a childish Joke

Oh Bollocks = The end of the world

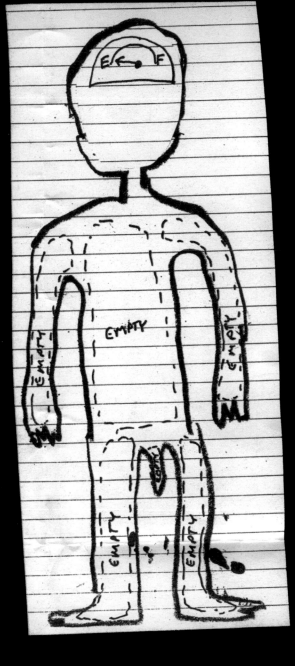

"Trust your intuition"

Fernando Gutierrez

Graphic Designer,
Partner, Pentagram
London

Born in London to Spanish parents,
Fernando Gutierrez studied graphic
design at the London College of
Printing. He began his career with
CDT Design in London before join-
ing Summa in Barcelona, where
he co-founded Grafica in 1993. In
October 2000, Fernando returned
to the UK as a partner at Pentagram
in London. As an art director,
Fernando also designs a wide variety
of magazines and newspapers,
exhibition catalogues, books, packaging, identities and exhibitions.
He was president of the European
Art Directors Club during 1998-99
and is a member of Alliance Graph-
ique Internationale and a fellow of
the Royal Society of Arts in London.

Inspiration

I'm inspired by the people I work with and I also find
dialogue inspiring.

Working environment

I'm not too fussy about my environment. As a designer,
you create environments. I never work from one and the
same space, but move around a lot and believe that my
ideal working environment travels with me. Where you
work isn't that important.
I surround myself with things I like, things that remind
me to do something, and they're always changing.
I always have books around me and magazines, newspapers, posters, packaging, wine bottles, a pirate flag,
a Michelin man and my chair. I love my chair – to sit in
but also just as an object.

Working process

I approach a job with a lot of questions. I do a lot of
research, but don't really have a routine. I try to be as
calm as possible and just work forwards so it evolves
and then just happens.
If you have a problem to crack and you're thinking about
it, ideas can come from anywhere at any time.

In the mornings, when I have a little distance to my
work, I have good ideas. Things seem really clear,
I have a good feeling, and then things take off. I rarely
get stuck.

I used to make sketchbooks. Now I keep notebooks,
mainly in written form.

Doing good work means being close to your clients,
which is why I go to Spain every two weeks.
Here at Pentagram you'll find a good archive, a good
library, good people and a good cook, which is
important.

Reading

I read *The Guardian, El Pais, The New Yorker* and
National Geographic, magazines such as *Another
Magazine* and *Dazed and Confused.*

Most inspiring person

Che Guevara, because he had an idea. What he represented and what he stood for were really interesting.

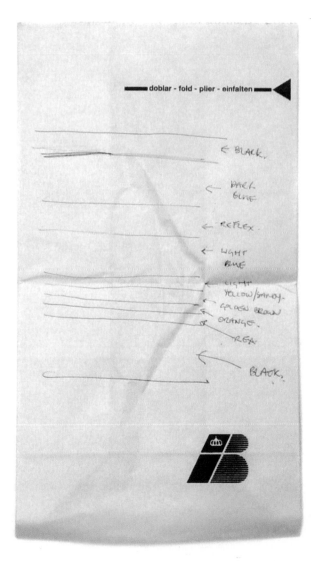

"Ideas can happen anywhere"

FERNANDO'S OFFICE AT PENTAGRAM
IN LONDON.

EL MUSEO DEL
PRADO

EL MUSEO DEL
PRADO

Fonds Mercator

EL PAIS

88   INS   GUTIERREZ

"My ideal working environment travels with me. Where I work isn't that important"

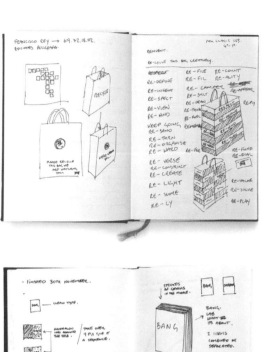

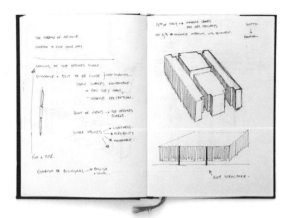

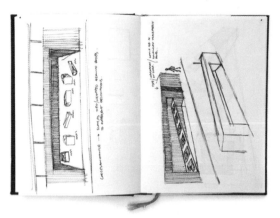

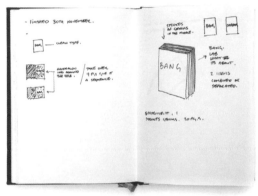

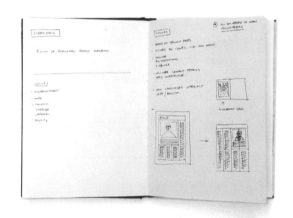

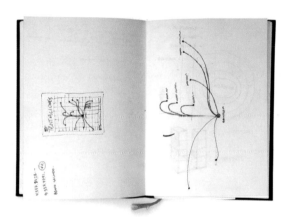

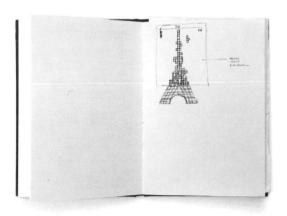

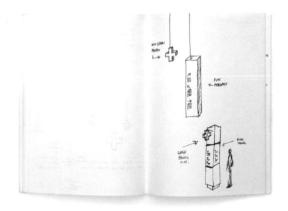

Henrik Juul
Creative Director,
Partner, People Group
Copenhagen

Born in Esbjerg, Denmark, Henrik
started his career at a small
local agency before attending
The Graphic Arts Institute of
Denmark and graduating in 1987.
He then joined Partners, a
Copenhagen advertising agency,
and started a career-long habit of
creating widely acclaimed and
memorable work. Over the years,
Henrik has created some of
Denmark's most famous
advertising, which has won him
international recognition at the
Cannes Advertising Festival and
Eurobest amongst others. He has
a list of Danish awards to his
name that is just as impressive,
and continues to be a strong
creative influence in his role as
creative director and partner of
People Group.

Inspiration
I find ordinary people very inspiring. Going to a supermarket is far more interesting workwise than reading
a lot of statistics. I also get a lot of inspiration from
my children. Children are great at making complicated
things simple.
I'm inspired mostly by real life. But of course also by
television, books and films. I like Bunuel, Truffaut,
The French New Wave, Avant-garde and British underground films. And I find The Simpsons, Allan Partridge
and The Office hilariously funny.
I don't do scrap or notebooks. I have never written
a note in my life. Instead I try to listen and focus on
capturing the essence.

Working environment
Two years ago I threw everything away. We were moving
our office, and I saw it as a chance to turn everything
upside down. Going from being personal to being more
professional. It was like a cleansing process throw-
ing away all the things you thought you had to have
around you when generating ideas. At the time it felt
quite strange and very scary. But today I enjoy starting
in a totally white room. It has taught me to be more
disciplined. It's a relief not to be dependent on physical
things. It's not important where you are. Instead, the
people you work with become more important.

Working process
I never do anything without a brief. It's almost like a
ritual. I read the brief, and then put it away, maybe for a
week, preferably longer. We do a lot of groundwork.
We interview the people that sell the product etc.
Anything may trigger the idea. Often it's a conversation.
Often, two or three words in the brief are the solution.
It's an intuitive thing.
I'm on call 24 hours a day. I can create whether I'm
in a good or a bad mood. I can always sit down and
write myself into the right frame of mind. I find that the
best concepts are often the ones that were difficult to
conceive.
I get my best ideas when I'm writing at home and
everybody else has gone to bed – between 10 pm and
2-3 in the morning. The more I write, the better it gets.
God is in the detail. When thinking, it's great to work
with others, but when I have to get ideas down on paper,
I prefer working on my own.

Reading
I don't read industry magazines. I prefer to find inspiration in the brief, rather than in other people's work.
I read lots of biographies. I find people that have meant
a lot to many people very interesting, odd personalities
like Hollywood producer Don Simpson, for instance.

Motivation
Trust. The fact that people come to you believing that
you can solve their problems. Doing something no one
has ever done before is also motivating.

Most inspiring person
My children.

"If you start with no invent everythin

thing, you have to
g from scratch"

Erik Kessels
Creative Director,
Founding Partner, KesselsKramer
Amsterdam

Erik Kessels is creative director
and co-founder of the Amsterdam-
based communication agency
KesselsKramer, which creates
memorable and award-winning
work for clients including Diesel,
Oxfam, Ben and The Hans Brinker
budget hotel. He is a passionate
collector of photographs and has
published several books of his
collected images: *Missing Link,
The Instant Men* and *In Almost
Every Picture*. Since 2000, he
has been editor of the alternative
photography magazine *Useful
Photography*. He organised the
exhibition *Dutch Delight* at
FOAM (Photography Museum
Amsterdam) and teaches
photography at the Gerrit
Rietveld Academy in Amsterdam.

Inspiration

I'm inspired by the environment here in the church.
I think it definitely stimulates creative thinking. When
we started KesselsKramer, we wanted to create a space
where you'd want to be and work. I don't understand
why some agencies seem to want to make their interiors
as boring as possible.
I also get a lot of inspiration from the street and from
art and photography. I find lectures really inspiring too.
I went to one of Saul Bass's last lectures in London and
it was fantastic to see him in action at the age of 60.
I sometimes just call people up that I'm interested in,
and try to meet them.
I teach photography at an art school here in Holland
and that also gives me an enormous amount of energy.

Working environment

The church vestry here at KesselsKramer is packed with
stuff from flea markets. I collect collections, like people's
old photo albums for example.
I also collect Polaroid cameras. I like being surrounded
by photographs.

Working process

I usually already have an idea in mind when I receive a
brief. It's intuitive and usually the best one in the end.
When you have to work too hard on an idea, it's usually
not so good. I think you also have to be a bit scared
about the decisions you make. It's important to challenge yourself and take risks.

The creatives are involved throughout the process. We
do research and try to define a territory. We never brain-
storm. I find it pointless.

I get my best ideas when I have the brief in my head and
sort of let it bounce around for a while. Then suddenly,
I get an idea. If I get stuck, I try not to think about it for
a while and not to worry.

Reading

I read *Permanent Food* and *Colours* magazine, especially
the issues in which they make an extreme choice, like
the whole issue devoted to one single person. I like that
idea. I like books such as *Kaddish* by Christian Boltanski,
The Art of Advertising by George Lois, *272 Pages* by
Hans-Peter Feldmann, *Double Game and Gotham
Handbook* by Sophie Calle, and *Tibor* by Tibor Kalman.

Motivation

I always want to make my work even better.

Most inspiring person

I think the artists and photographers who inspire
me the most are: Christian Boltanski, Hans-Peter
Feldmann, Sol Lewitt, John Baldesarri, Lee Friedlander,
Garry Winogrand, Sophie Calle, Mauricio Cattelan,
Barbara Kruger, Daido Moriyama, Jenny Holtzer, Hans
van der Meer, Hans Aarsman and Ed van der Elsken.
The most inspiring people within music are: Steve Reich,
Ryuichi Sakamoto, Smashing Pumpkins, Motörhead
and Queens of Stoneage.

"I collect collections"

"I don't understand why
want to make their interi

some agencies seem to

ors as boring as possible"

KESSELSKRAMER'S OFFICE IN A
FORMER CHURCH IN AMSTERDAM.

"I collect Polaroid cameras and always carry one with me"

Marlene Anine Kjær
Fashion design student,
Danmarks Designskole
Copenhagen

Marlene was born in 1975.
She is studying Fashion Design at
Danmarks Designskole and will
graduate in 2006. Her ambition is
to become a fashion designer with
a difference.

Inspiration

I'm inspired by society, by nature, people, shapes,
beauty and aesthetics. I paint, draw and make collages
and do a lot of photography.
I keep scrapbooks because they are great for ideas when
you're going through a dry spell. I keep packaging, bags,
wrapping paper, pictures and coins. You can't really call
it a collection. It's more like a stockpile.
Sometimes I use what I call 'inspiration on command'.
I pick a random thing that I have to use. It could be a
stone, a twig or anything else – as long as it gives me a
new angle.

Working environment

Setting up my workspace is important to me. For each
project I arrange it differently, depending on the nature
of the project. I always start with an empty desk. There
has to be room for mess and enough space so that I
can work on different things at the same time. It's fun
to see how my desk develops during the process. It's
surrounded by boards where I stick my visual starting
points – the essence of what I'm working on.
I also surround myself with scrapbooks, colour samples,
tools and a sewing machine.

Working process

I do a lot of thinking before starting work on a new
project or collection. It's important to choose the right
starting point and establish an interesting universe. If I
start out wrong, I feel it all the way through the project.

I get my best ideas when I'm not expecting them. Often
at awkward times, like just before I'm going to sleep. Or
in the strangest places: when I'm peeling carrots or talking about tonsillitis. The project I'm working on always
seems to be simmering in the back of my mind.
If I get stuck, I either focus on the end result and work
my way through, or I do something completely different,
like painting, drawing or taking photographs. I might
start collecting things I find inspiring and interesting,
and let them stimulate new ideas.
I create a book or sketchbook for each new project.
It's a tool that follows the project and the process, and
helps define how things fit together. Then I can steer
very precisely through a project as it progresses. I can
see when something is getting out of hand, or when
something works really well.

Reading

I read novels and reference books. I like books that are
very visual and have lots of pictures of furniture, art or
a particular style for example, or a period such as the
Bauhaus era.

Motivation

My motivation is to create beautiful, aesthetic things.
I try not to intellectualise too much, as it destroys my
motivation for creating clothes.

Most inspiring person

Victor & Rolf.

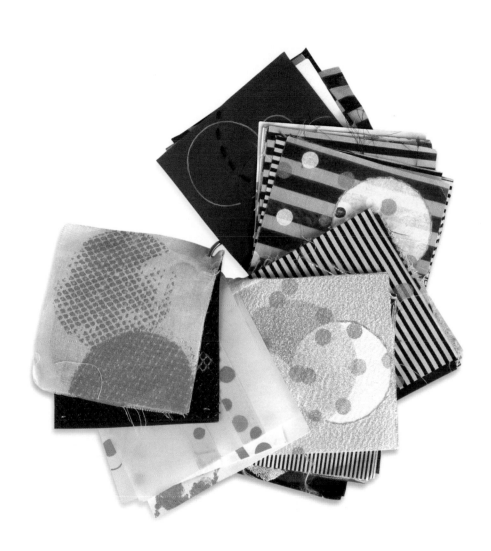

"I create idea banks"

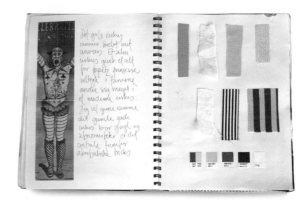

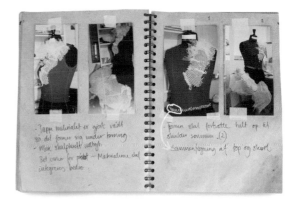

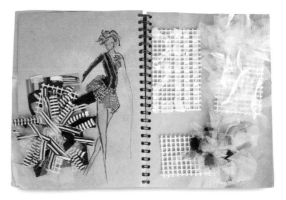

Filippa Knutsson
Founder and Creative
Director of Filippa K
Stockholm

Born in Stockholm in 1965,
Filippa grew up in England, where
she went on to study fashion at
the American College in London.
She returned to her native Sweden
to work for the family fashion
business, Gul&Blå. In 1993 Filippa
co-founded Filippa K together with
partners Patrik Kihlborg and Karin
Segerblom. 1997 saw the launch
of her first collection of women's
jerseys, knitwear and jeans through
selected retailers in Sweden.
The Filippa K label continued to
develop and expand and in the
same year, the company opened its
first two stores in Sweden. Her work
has won her numerous awards,
including the prestigious Swedish
fashion award "Guldknappen"
(The Golden Button).

Inspiration

I love travelling. Discovering new countries, cultures
and environments stimulates my brain and gives me
an enormous feeling of freedom. It also creates a calm
within me and allows space for creativity.
The design team and I often go on inspiration trips.
Partly to get inspiration, but also to do something
together and to exchange ideas and thoughts.
Meetings with people also inspire me, but I think the
most important inspiration comes from within yourself.

Working environment

We have a big airy studio. I spend some of my time
there, but I don't have a fixed spot. I don't even have a
desk. I move around all the time. I don't like the idea of
having a desk filled with paper. It makes me stressed.
I try not to spend too much time in the office, as I need
to have a certain distance and freedom. I work partly
from home, especially if I have to write something.
I do a lot of writing. I think it's in my nature to express
myself verbally and in writing.
I don't use notebooks or sketchpads. I've tried, but
I always lose them. They're either too small or too big.
I'm too impatient. I find putting things down on paper
too limiting and restricting. I do have a laptop though.
I like it because I can clean out, edit and erase very
easily. I'm not a collector, I don't like the idea of collecting. I always throw things away.

Working process

When I start working on a new collection, I have to be
on my own. I think and I visualise. I use my inner eye. I
believe that ideas come to you if you trust that they will.

You can't force the process. It's like with colours; I've
never been able to explain how it happens, but they just
come to me... kind of from inside. I also get together
with the whole team, but then I need to have prepared
myself first. To get into the right frame of mind, I have to
be calm and rested. I need peace and quiet around me.
I love being busy and having a lot of projects running at
the same time, but I hate chaos and disorder.
I meditate. I think it's important to take care of yourself,
and to create peace around you. A massage is also great.
Often the best ideas come when I switch everything off,
for instance when I'm on holiday. If I get stuck, I discuss
the project with others. It's important to talk, be honest
and not to be precious about ideas. There's a good
atmosphere around here, we have a fantastic, dedicated
team and ideas can come from anyone.

Motivation

When I started off, it was a need to prove myself, and
show that I could succeed. Today it's something else:
achieving my goals and dreams, and succeeding with
my ideas.

Reading

I usually don't have enough time to read. But when I do,
I read a lot. I read the *Herald Tribune* in the mornings.
I grew up in London and it's important for me to still
keep in touch with Europe and the world. Other than
that, I read books with positive life-affirming messages.

Most inspiring person

In the world of fashion: Donna Karan. She's always been
true to herself and her ideas.

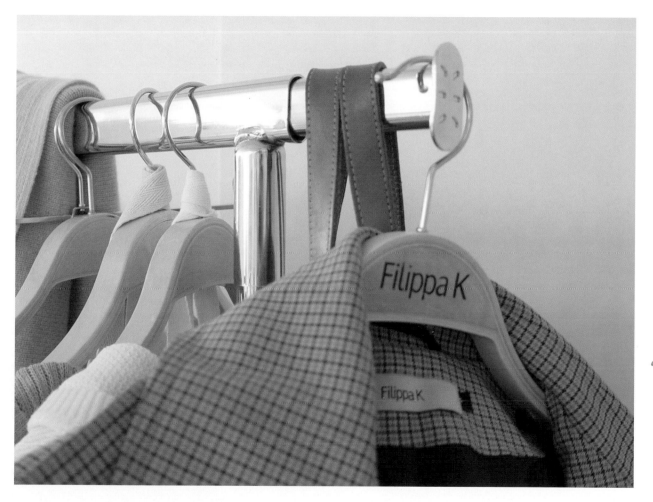

"I like working conceptually. I'm always thinking about the bigger picture, and don't like getting stuck in details"

"I don't have a desk. I move around all
the time. I don't like the idea of having
a desk filled with paper"

S 06
WOMAN

Salesman
samples

Produktions ex.

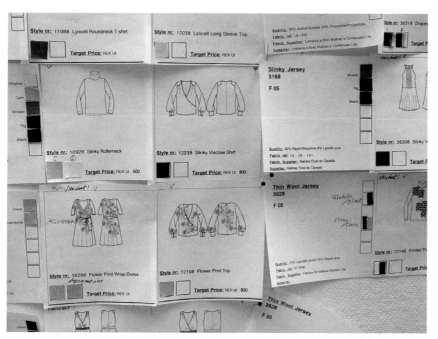

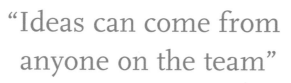

"Ideas can come from anyone on the team"

Otto Kruijssen
Artist, VJ
Amsterdam

Born in 1969, Otto studied at the Rietveld Akademie in Amsterdam before starting to paint professionally in 1993. He has exhibited at Go Gallery and Gallery Rudolvf, Amsterdam, Vips Gallery, Rotterdam, Tentententoonstelling, Netherlands, Jet-set Club, St. Petersburg and Festival Celimontana, Rome. He has had commissions from Heineken, Ford, Microsoft, Mercedes and Mars amongst others. He also VJ's at Las Palmas, Supperclub, NOW&WOW, Off Corso and Paradiso in the Netherlands.

Inspiration
I'm inspired by greatness. I find it inspiring when people make really amazing stuff – a movie, music, a work of art, anything – as long as it amazes you.

Working environment
I'd like to say I surround myself with as little as possible. I try to keep very few distractions around me. But it doesn't seem to work.
I collect paintings by other people. I also collect souvenirs, toys, little statues and everyday packaging in foreign languages. I have boxes full in my studio.
I don't go to my studio to get ideas. Most of the time I have the ideas ready, either in my head or in my sketchbook.

Working process
I play the same song all day to get in the right frame of mind. I get rid of distractions and switch off the phone. I just work and work and work... then all of a sudden I have a series of paintings. I don't plan it. Actually, the first thing I do is buy the right size canvas. That's where the work starts. Sometimes I have a picture in my head when I start, and sometimes I have no idea at all.
I get my best ideas in crazy places: in the car, on my bicycle or in the shower. I used to keep a waterproof marker in the shower to write things on the walls. Then I copied them down in a sketchbook later. I also get a lot of ideas in bed. In the hours between going to bed and falling asleep. I always keep a sketchbook around. It can be really annoying to wake up and have to get out of bed to write things down, but I do. I think it's really important to record such ideas. Sometimes I have really visual ideas, like a complete image. And sometimes just ideas about things to do.
You wouldn't think so, but I'm totally precious about my sketchbooks – but on the other hand I really like it when other people draw in them. They are always full of drawings by other artists, friends and kids.

I don't do any commercial work any more. Combining that with my personal work was a mess.
If I get stuck when I'm working, I destroy the painting and start over again, or paint over it. Sometimes I leave paintings unfinished for a year. That's one of the difficult things: finishing things off.
I'm really interested in the process of painting. Painters work mostly on their own, but I thought it could be fun to see how other people work. So I started the 'Kwasten met Gasten' project, where I paint together with other artists. Watching other people paint is one of my favourite things in the world.

Motivation
I'm still really interested in the whole process. Every time it's different. I always manage to surprise myself. I just love painting, and the smell of paint.

Reading
I read history books about all the wars since 1914. I never read art or design books. I don't want to get influenced too much.

Most inspiring person
Ronald Reagan is fascinating. The guy was one of the craziest people to run the world. He was insane.

"I do get stuck, but only because I have too many ideas"

115

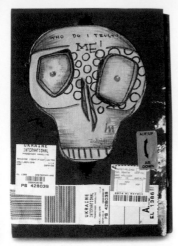

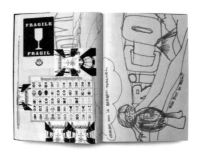

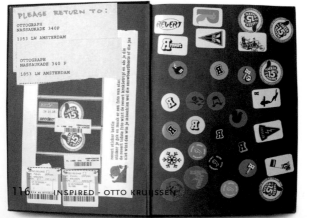

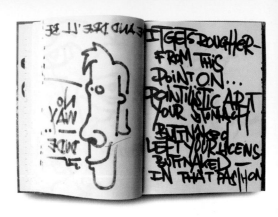

"I'm totally precious about my sketchbooks – but on the other hand I really like it when other people draw in them"

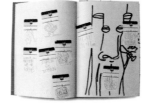

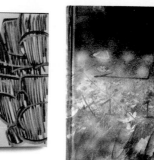

INSPIRED - OTTO KRUISSEN

OTTO'S STUDIO IN AN ABANDONED
SUPERMARKET IN AMSTERDAM.

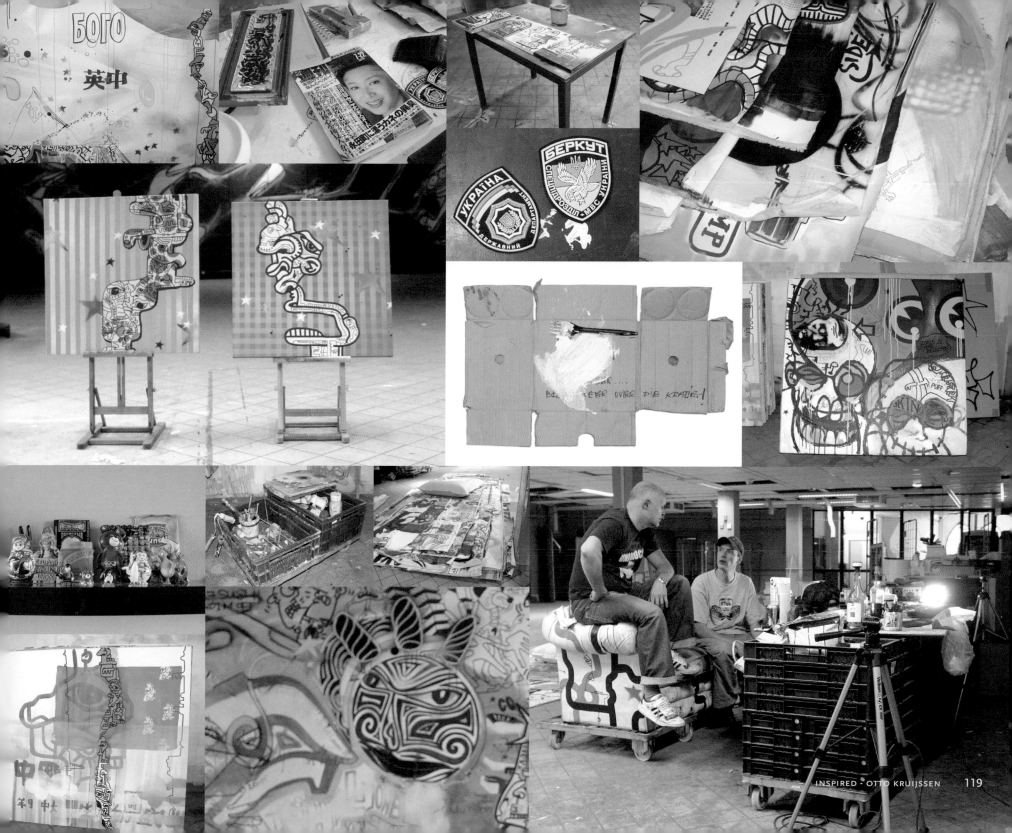

"I love stickers,
they remind
me of my
graffiti past"

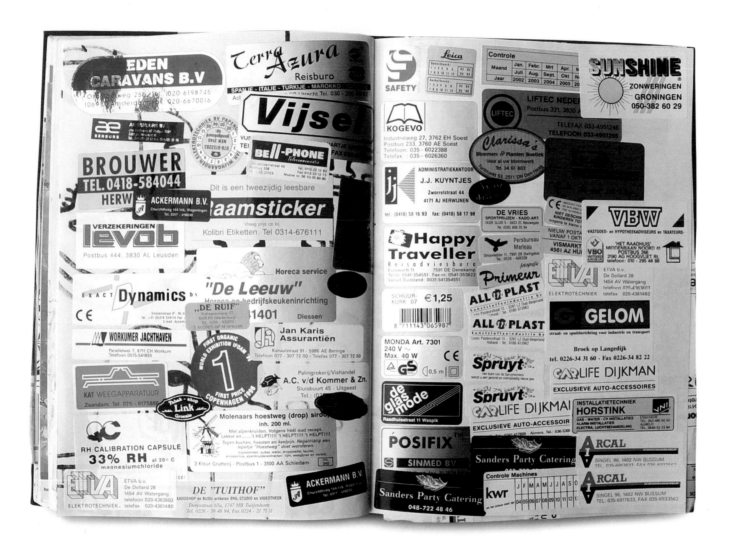

Anders Lund Madsen

Entertainer
Copenhagen

Anders was born in 1963 in the
small Danish town of Mørkhøj.
Since graduating from The Danish
School of Journalism in 1990,
he has pursued a varied and very
successful career as, amongst other
things, a comedian, entertainer,
public speaker, writer, television
presenter and circus director.

Inspiration

When I panic, inspiration seems to come to me, then
things start to happen. Otherwise, it can be something
I hear, something I read, or something that creates an
image in my mind. I'm inspired by real life. The fantastic
moments in life, where reality somehow seems to be
jolted out of place.
I enjoy sitting down where there is a lot of action, like
in a restaurant, a harbour or a café. I use notebooks
for writing, doodling and sketching. I don't collect anything. I leave keeping scrapbooks and clippings to my
mother-in-law.

Working environment

I get all my best ideas when submerged in water. I've
had a bath at least once a day, every day, since leaving
high school. The hotter the water, the better the ideas.
I actually bought my house because of the bathtub.

Working process

I make a living from making people laugh. When asked
what I do, I normally answer: I turn moods around.
When I start a show, I don't know what's going to
happen. I find connections between my audience and
my material on the spot. The less research and fewer
rehearsals I do, the more fun it is.
I trust in the moment. If I stop respecting that, it just
doesn't happen. Then it's like one long free fall, a jump
without a parachute. Bang!

I'm very brave. I'm not worried about losing face. Still
I'm always nervous until I get the first laugh. Sometimes
it feels like standing on the edge of the abyss, and then
you realise that you can fly. Sometimes it feels as if the
audience is as relieved as I am. You get a lot of goodwill
and ego boosting out of it.

I have a well-developed feeling for situations. I rely on
my talent for compassion and my gift for generating
knowledge and communicating it. I try to be entertaining, funny and relevant. I make my audience happy and
cheerful, without patting them on the head. I have three
rules; I musn't touch them physically, lie to them, or be
a brown nose.

You have to be relaxed about ideas. Get them out, air
them. The more ideas you give away, the better the ideas
you'll get in return.

Motivation

Providing for my family.

Reading

I read a lot; magazines, newspapers, stuff I find on the
internet, books, particularly novels and books about
the brain. I watch hardly any television.

Most inspiring person

My eight-year-old daughter Björk.

"I get my best ideas when submerged in water. The hotter the water, the better the ideas"

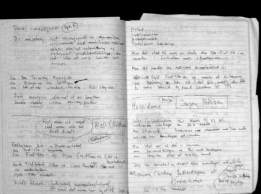
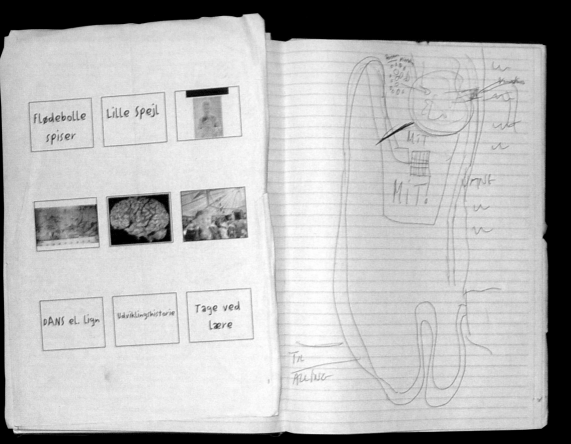

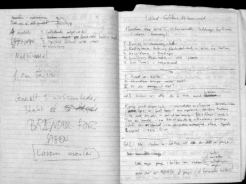
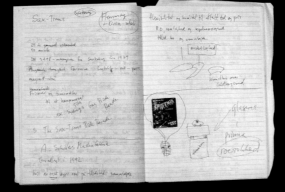
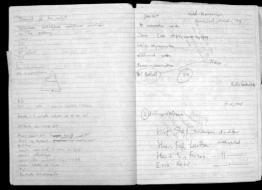

> "The more ideas you give away, the better the ideas you'll get in return"

Vicki Maquire

Senior Copywriter, DLKW
London

Vicki graduated with a degree in
fashion design from Newcastle
University and continued her career
working in a variety of creative set-
tings as a journalist and window
dresser before exploring the field
of public relations. In 1993, she
started in advertising and went on
to become an award-winning copywriter. She has recently returned
from the Mojo Sydney advertising
agency in Australia and is now a
senior copywriter at DLKW, London.

Inspiration

Sitting on beautiful sand, watching a beautiful sunset,
surrounded by beautiful people... I couldn't think of a
bloody thing. Now I've swapped Bondi Beach, Sydney
for Bethnal Green, London and I'm loving every pol-
luted, foul smelling, run down minute of it. So for
inspiration I'd have to say: colour, chaos, noise, dirt,
cities and mad people.

Working environment

I try to surround myself with people who are funnier,
more talented and cleverer than I am in the hope it'll rub
off. When they're not around, it's books, music, things
that make me laugh and the TV.
I try to work in an environment where there is always
something to distract me from the task in hand.
I collect other people's sketchbooks and scrapbooks.

Working process

To get into the right frame of mind, I skirt around the
brief until I've cultivated the right balance of fear and
excitement to sit down and tackle it.
I don't know why, but I do my best thinking on the toilet.
If I get stuck for an idea, I write everything down that's
in my head. Hopefully a good idea will move into that
empty space.

Reading

I'll read anything that's to hand, except for the *Sunday
Times*. Art magazines from the sixties, old copies of *Viz*,
anything by Spike Milligan, old copies of *The Leicester
Mercury* and *The Sun*.

Most inspiring person

My mum... standing on Leicester market selling
bric-a-brac on a freezing January morning.

"I try to surround myself with people who are funnier, more talented and cleverer than I am, in case it'll rub off"

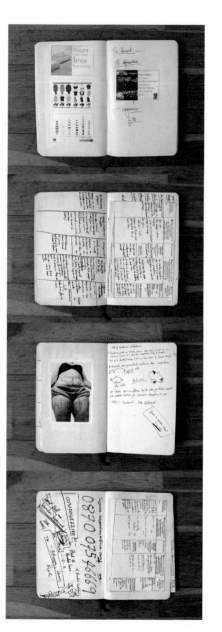

"I do my best thinking on the toilet"

Paul Neale
Graphic Designer, Founder of
Graphic Thought Facility
London

Born in Leicestershire in 1966,
Paul studied Graphic Design at
Saint Martins School of Art and
the Central School of Art and Design,
and later at the Royal College of Art.
He is a founding member of
Graphic Thought Facility (GTF) in
London, whose clients include
the Design Museum, Victoria &
Albert Museum, Shakespeare's
Globe Theatre, Habitat, Manchester
City Art Galleries, Booth-Clibborn
Editions, Selfridges, National Glass
Centre, the Tate Gallery, Antoni +
Alison, the London College of
Printing, Royal College of Art,
the Natural History Museum, the
Science Museum and the Institute
for Contemporary Art. Paul also
lectured in typography and design
at Central Saint Martins from
1991–1996.

Inspiration
We always work with a problem. Always. So the problem has to be inspiring. Inspiration can come from the client's needs, or from the problem itself. There's always something in there. Simultaneously we also design backwards – from the point of manufacture, visiting manufacturers so we can design efficiently and economically. Talking to them can be very inspiring. I'm also inspired by other areas of design, art, technology and processes.

Working environment
I spend more time in the company of those people I work with than anyone else, so it's important that the environment is right. Unlike our last studio, we now have enough space to work comfortably and efficiently – a large table where we can all sit and talk, a space where you can spread things out…

I surround myself with lots of stuff. Boxes of crap. I keep visual reference, notebooks and boxes of ephemera. I prefer boxes to scrapbooks, because many of the things I keep are three-dimensional.

I collect records, books, printed stuff… but I try not to start new collections. Collecting is such a male trait. I keep references to things I want to remember. I find that if I keep something – although I might never look at it again – it's somehow stored in my mind, ready to be used someday.

Working process
We often approach a new job by sitting round the table having a discussion together. That's how a lot of ideas start. Dialogue helps push your ideas forward quickly – working out what's good/bad, what's valid/invalid. I also think problems through on my own. My bath is the best place for clear thinking. Some baths are very long. I sketch starting points (often on wet pieces of paper) – just enough to articulate an idea to other studio members.
Any reccurring visual style in our work comes out of our process of working through and rationalising the problem.

Clearing my desk can also help me get into the right frame of mind when there's a new job to be thought about. I like to start a new job by clearing my desk. Tidy desk, tidy mind.

Reading
I read newspapers, rock biographies and music encyclopaedia. I rarely read fiction, and I don't go to the cinema much. I watch too much trash telly.

Motivation
I'm motivated by wanting to do new stuff and make things happen.

Most inspiring person
Probably my mother's father. He died when I was 10, but he sewed a lot of seeds in my brain.

GRAPHIC THOUGHT FACILITY'S
STUDIO IN LONDON.

Barbro Ohlson Smith
Graphic Designer
Stockholm

Barbro started her design career in London in 1989 with Carroll Dempsey & Thirkell. In 1994, she co-founded Persona Design, working for clients in both London and Stockholm before making the move to Sweden as head of art direction at Berghs School of Communication and later as head of graphic design and creative director at the Swedish Television Channel TV4. Barbro now runs her own design consultancy, Ohlsonsmith in Stockholm.

Inspiration
I get my inspiration from people with interesting ideas, new thoughts and striking work. Also nature, jewellery, furniture, photography, contemporary dance, art and sculptures. My favourite design period is the sixties, and I also find that Japanese design inspires me.

Working environment
I surround myself with images, type, stones, things with special textures, fabric, flowers. I love string, yarns and cottons of all kinds. I'm an avid collector of jewellery, handbags and stones. Postcards, tickets, menus and things like that are also great and they all end up in boxes and folders. Wherever I work, I create a 'gallery' of interesting things around me. The atmosphere of a workspace is important to me. A beautiful space clears my thoughts.

Working process
A good 'ritual' for me when starting a new project is to clean my desk and create some space, both physically and mentally. I usually get my best ideas when I have a moment to myself. That can be on the bus or when taking a walk. Sometimes the idea pops up after days of research and inspiration, in unexpected surroundings. When I work, I start by researching the assignment. Sometimes I create mood boards or just collect images and things. I sketch first. The computer always comes last.

If I get stuck, I try to change my environment, go for a walk, talk and discuss the problem with people around me.
I really enjoy working in collaboration with others to develop an idea or design. I get very excited and get a real thrill out of the process.

Reading
I love books and I spend a lot of time in contemporary and antiquarian bookshops.
I read mainly by 'looking' at images and typography rather than reading traditionally, except when I read fiction or research material.

Motivation
My motivation lies in the ability to help other people to communicate their messages.
Giving a project, company or a product its visual voice, a relevant voice. I really believe that everything communicates something. So there is much to be done for the total experience of how we perceive a message, a person, a product or a company.
For me, the process of designing is never the same. I'm always optimistic that 'this time it'll be brilliant'.

Most inspiring person
There are many, but for their work I'd say choreographer and dancer Akram Khan, 'total designer' Bruno Munari and photographer Nick Knight.

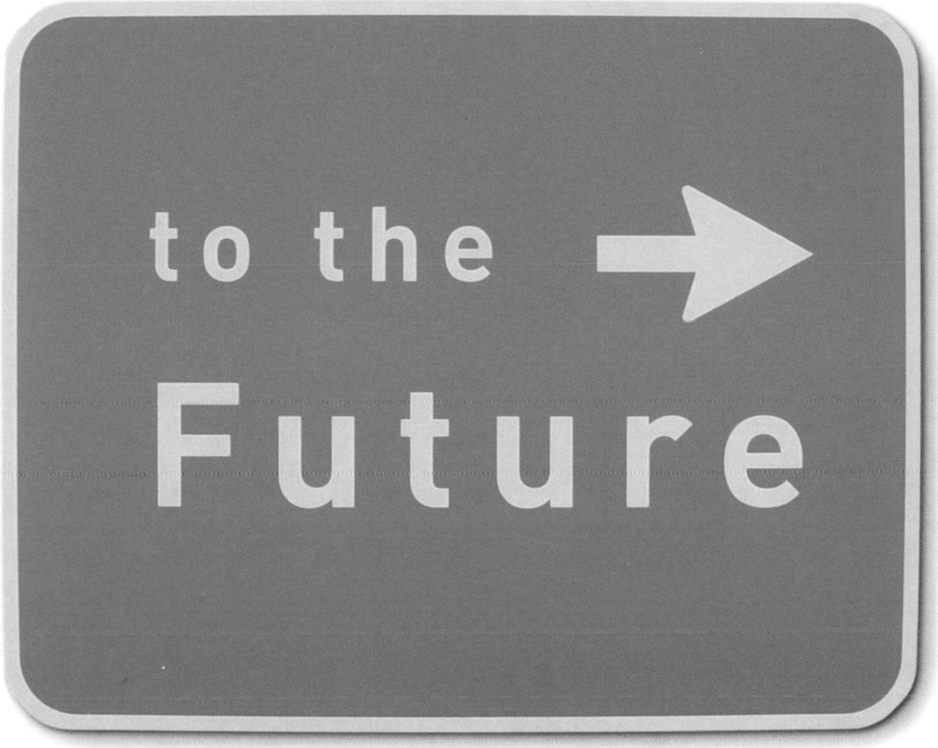
to the
Future

"Everything communicates"

Erwin Olaf
Photographer
Amsterdam

Erwin was born in 1959 in Hilversum
in The Netherlands. After graduating
from the School of Journalism in
1980, he started working as a
journalistic photographer. As his
career developed, he was frequently
commissioned for magazine work,
and by film and record companies.
His work has been exhibited on
numerous occasions and he has created award-winning work for brands
such as Nokia, Diesel and Levi's.

Erwin Olaf portrait by Feriet Tunc.

Inspiration
I organise parties to get inspired. The nightlife scene has
always fascinated me. The human body also inspires me.

Working environment
Silence is the most important feature of my working
environment.

Working process
I approach a job with an empty head and open mind.
I withdraw and reflect to get myself in the right frame
of mind. For assignments, you only really have to react
to the client's original idea and bounce ideas back and
forth. The work I do on commissioned assignments
inspires my own personal work and vice versa.
If I get stuck, I take a moment to reflect.
When I've just finished a major exhibition, I need time
to recharge my batteries, like right now for example,
and I do that by consuming art, films, books etc. I usually
get my best ideas when I'm on holiday, on the beach.

Reading
I don't seem to have time for that anymore. I never
read magazines. I actually don't like fashion or fashion
magazines.

Motivation
Fear of boredom definitely keeps me going.

Most inspiring people
Andy Warhol and Hans van Manen (Dutch ballet
choreographer).

ERWIN OLAF IN HIS STUDIO
IN AMSTERDAM.

MIND YOUR HEAD

THE PHOTOGRAPH 'CHILL OUT'
WAS INSPIRED BY THE 'FUCQUE
LES BALLES' PARTY.

© ERWIN OLAF

"I organise parties to get inspiration"

Rodrigo Otazu
Jewellery Designer,
Founder of Otazu
Amsterdam

Rodrigo was born in Buenos Aires, Argentina. While travelling the world as a model for Calvin Klein, Rodrigo found inspiration in Sydney and created his first necklace, which was featured in the Australian edition of Vogue. Rodrigo then settled in Amsterdam, where he opened his own studio. Soon he was commissioned to design couture pieces for several shows. Rodrigo's collections not only became an instant success with buyers and the press, they also attracted support from numerous high profile celebrities. He has successfully expanded his own distinctive brand of jewellery in over twenty countries worldwide and has collaborated with Gassan Diamonds, Christian Lacroix and Clements Ribeiro, amongst others.

Inspiration
Life and love inspire me.

Working environment
I surround myself with books, trust and love. Good taste is important to me. I love working on my own with music and candles. I have a house in Bali where I often go when working on collections.

Working process
I approach a job by closing my eyes and visualising it. I do a lot of research, absorb information and read. Then I play around with pieces and it evolves.
My best ideas come from life. I don't know what 'not working' is. I work all the time, so my ideas always come at strange moments. I recently created a whole collection while on a short break in Marrakesh.
I never get stuck, touch wood. I believe that every problem has a solution. You just have to deal with it. I sketch, do scrapbooks, use 3D programs on the computer, the internet and e-mail.
I refuse to get stuck in my way of working. If I get bored, it's over. I collect books, books and books – about fashion, art, craft, anything.

Motivation
Love.

Reading
I read the Dalai Lama. He's a soul cleaner.

Most inspiring person
My mother. She was also an artist and taught me about staying true to myself. And then I admire people as different as Madonna, Viktor & Rolf, Galliano and the photographer Fritz Kok.
I'm fascinated by popularity, fame and money, and by the lives of Marilyn Monroe, Charlie Chaplin, Nelson Mandela and Jackie O.

"I'm more of an entertainer than a designer"

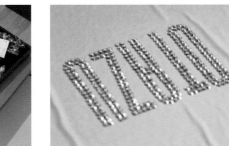

"I need fascination"

Chris Priest

Typographer
London

After attending Bournville College of Art and being awarded the Everyman Award for Graphic Design in 1986, Chris continued his education at Saint Martins School of Art. He began his design career at Why Not Associates in 1990, and in 1993 was featured in Creative Review magazine's prestigious Creative Futures showcase. He continued to develop and diversify as a freelance designer before setting up his own studio, Barbara, in 1996. In 1998, Chris joined Ogilvy and Mather in London, where he applied his creative talent to many global brands. Chris has lectured at the Society of Typographic Designers, Saint Martins, the Bourneville and Watford Colleges of Art and has been featured in many publications and design annuals. He DJs when he can, and is a green belt in Shokatan karate.

Inspiration

I love street culture, graffiti and the surf culture. I think surfboards and skateboards are great for inspiration. I keep scrapbooks, idea books and clippings. For me a scrapbook is like a visual development diary, a personal journey. I use them for visual reference and for creative development. I see them as a part of the creative process. I think making scrapbooks creates confidence in your visual language. When you're actually working on them, sticking things down, you explore space, tension and composition. I use glue, staples, anything. It's like a journey from cover to cover.

I'm inspired by the chaos theory, universal energy and the butterfly effect. The universe is chaotic in a divine, orderly way.

Working environment

Music is very important, but it has to be right. My rollups are very important. Volvic is very important. It tastes much better than Evian.

I collect lots of things. I remember that the first things I started collecting were sugar packets from aeroplanes... and that was when my mother started to worry! Now I collect music, any shape or form of packaging, stuff, anything. I have a passion for animals, especially buffalos. I have a large collection of miniature buffalos.

Working process

I approach every job differently. But I always start on a piece of paper. I sketch. I doodle. As to how I get my best ideas, there's no order to it. I look at something and almost instinctively I see how it should be. I'm eternally grateful. I think it's a gift. Sometimes I feel my day has come. I've run out of ideas and can't think of anything. Then I go away. I take some time off. I get myself out of it. If you're open enough, your inspiration can come from anywhere.

Motivation

I have an innate passion for creativity. I'm actually no good at anything else.

Most inspiring person

Bob Marley.

"For me a scrapbook
is like a visual
development diary,
a personal journey"

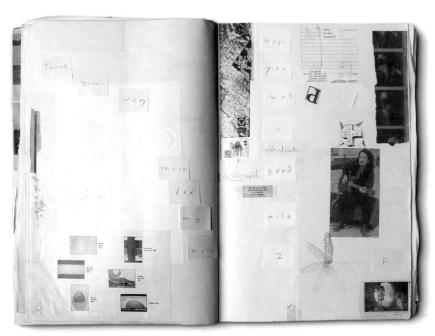

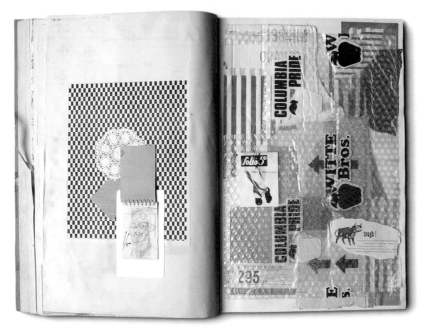

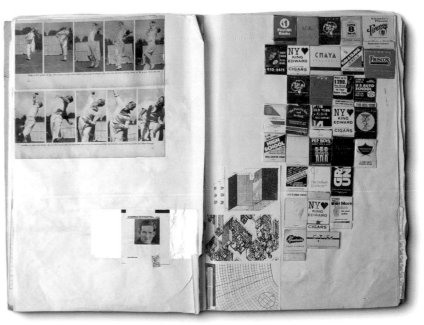

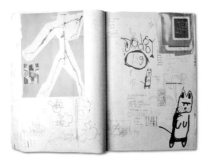

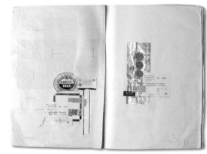

"I've always surrounded myself with lots of things"

Ingegerd Råman
Product- and Glassware Designer,
Potter, Stockholm

Born in 1943 in Stockholm, Ingegerd
is considered one of Sweden's most
distinguished glassware designers.
She was educated at the University
College of Arts, Crafts and Design
in Stockholm and the Instituto
Statale D'Arte per la Ceramica in
Faenza, Italy. Her work has been
commissioned by the Swedish
Ministry for Foreign Affairs, the
Swedish Royal Court and Trussardi,
amongst others. Her designs have
been displayed in museums, design
boutiques and galleries worldwide.
She is represented at the Victoria
and Albert Museum, London, the
Stedelijk Museum, Amsterdam, the
Corning Museum of Glass, USA and
the National Art Gallery, Stockholm.
Her work has also won her many
distinguished awards, including
The Prince Eugen Medal given by
His Majesty The King of Sweden.
In 1995, the Swedish Government
appointed her honorary professor.

Inspiration
I find inspiration in many different things: a meeting
or a colour, in music or art. Where and how I find it, is
almost always a coincidence. I also find other people's
needs inspiring. The objects I create are always useful.
It could be a particular object that I myself would like to
have. I'm always my first customer.

Working environment
For my workshop in the south of Sweden, the brief to
the architects was very simple: everything had to be
hidden behind cupboard doors. It creates a serene
environment where I can work well.
My ideal environment is light, empty and organised.
I dream of sitting in an empty room with only whatever
I'm working on in front of me. But I work with small
three-dimensional objects, so they're everywhere.
When I'm in the workshop, I don't want anyone else
around. I'm a social animal, but I need solitude when
I'm working.
Usually I haven't got any music or the radio on. I like
it to be quiet. When I do play music, I tend to play the
same song over and over again, which drives other
people crazy.
I'm not a collector. I love things, but I don't want to
have them around me.

Working process
I start a new project by doing a lot of thinking. I work
mainly with mouth-blown glass. I don't blow it myself,
I only make 2-D sketches, like silhouettes. Then I add
notes with the exact specifications for the 3-D aspect.

It's the details that make my objects unique.
If I'm working with a new type of material, I always
start with a visit to the factory to get to know that
particular material better. Then the material becomes
my starting point.
I sketch on greaseproof paper that I buy cheap from
the supermarket. It's not intimidating, you can make
mistakes without feeling that you've ruined the paper.
I started doing this when I was a student and couldn't
afford anything better, but now I prefer it.
The paper goes yellow and disintegrates after a couple
of years – an idea I quite like. I don't want any sketches
to be left when I'm gone.
I usually get my best ideas when I'm not thinking of
anything. Then my brain works the hardest. Walking gets
me in the right frame of mind. I walk for an hour every
day. Things fall into place when the body is moving.
My biggest asset, but also the thing I find hardest, is
finding time. I need lots of time in the design process.
For a designer there's no difference between your private
life and your working life.

Motivation
I have a passion for design. I'm very disciplined. I work
every day and I'm always busy with something. Passion
drives me.

Reading
I read fiction, but never by Swedish authors. I imagine
that if I read foreign books I'll see things in a different
way and get a glimpse into other cultures and ways
of thinking.

"I sketch on greaseproof paper that I buy cheap from the supermarket. It's not intimidating, you can make mistakes without feeling that you've ruined the paper"

"The best designed product is the one that hasn't been invented yet"

MEZZO
II

"I'm always my first customer.
If I can't imagine having
or using a particular object,
I won't design it either"

Vibeke Rohland
Textile Designer
Copenhagen

From 1978–82, Vibeke studied at
the Institute for the History of Art
at Copenhagen University before
studying Textile Design at Danmarks
Designskole. After graduating
in 1986, Vibeke has pursued a
successful career in textile design,
exhibiting at the Danish Design
Centre, Charlottenborg, Museum
of Industrial Art, Museum of Art
at Bremen, Nordjyllands Museum
of Art, Neue Sammlung Berlin,
Danish Centre for Architecture,
Kunstforeningen Gl. Strand, Esbjerg
Museum of Art, Borås Museum
of Art, Centre for Danish Painting,
and Scotsdale Arizona.
She has had design work commis-
sioned by such clients as Esprit,
DSB, Fischer+Design, Paustian,
Baby Tata – New York, IKEA, Abc
Carpet and Home – New York,
Bodum, TV Zulu, Netto,
Georg Jensen, and Hay.

Inspiration

I find inspiration in all sorts of places. In supermarkets,
the street, talking to people, travelling to China or sitting
with both legs up, reading fashion magazines.
I sketch and draw a lot. I keep sketchbooks, idea books
and diaries. I'm not precious about my sketchbooks. I
make them for myself and they are a mix of seriousness
and humour.

I keep loads of things: colour samples, pieces of text,
letters, postal stamps, X-rays, packaging, Chinese
lettering and newspapers, patterns, price tags, scraps of
fabric, magazine clippings, business cards, milk bottles,
buttons and oilcloths. I keep all these things, because
I think they are great, but don't ask me what I'm going
to use them for. They are all starting points, and can
lead to anything. If there's something I particularly like,
it ends up on the wall. It can be anything magical, an
unusual colour, or something that means something
special to me.

Working environment

It has to be clean and tidy. I like working in organised
chaos. Fresh air is also important. I always keep
the door or a window open when I work. I love being
surrounded by beautiful things and colours.

Working process

In the morning I run. I always have a lot of energy and
running gets me into the right frame of mind. When I
get to my workshop, I turn on the music straight away.
Then I begin by looking for a good starting point.
My best ideas can be triggered by anything: a sentence,
a colour, a movie or an old tea towel. The best ideas are
simple and unique. I love creating useful objects, such
as tea towels, bed linen and T-shirts. And I enjoy doing
large-scale projects with a more conceptual angle.
If I get stuck, I jump on my bike, go shopping, or start
cleaning up. Sometimes I print; I prepare a piece of
fabric and start in the left-hand corner. I create a shape,
take a look, and then create another one, then I repeat
it. I love repetition.
I've never found it hard to work on my own. Much of
the time I seem to be doing a lot without really knowing
what it will be used for. I'm always working.

Reading

I love newspapers. I read everything from financial
papers and the business pages to *National Geographic*,
or special-offer leaflets – they are great for knowing
what's happening out there. It's about people and what
they surround themselves with. I read books, especially
historical and reference books.

Motivation

I don't know what else to do. For me there's no such
thing as a day off. I love what I do, and do it all the time.
The older I get, the braver I become. But it takes time.
I believe that if you want to be good at what you do,
it takes time.

"If there's something I really like, it ends up on the wall"

INSPIRED - VIBEKE ROHLAND

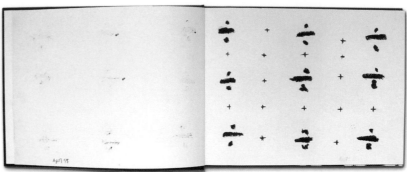

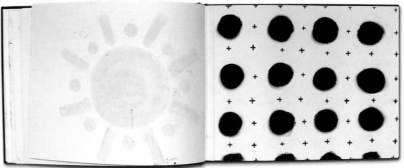

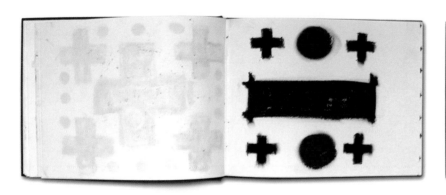

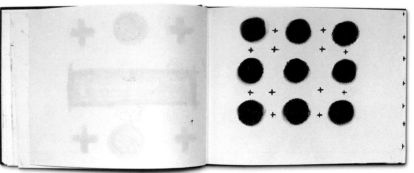

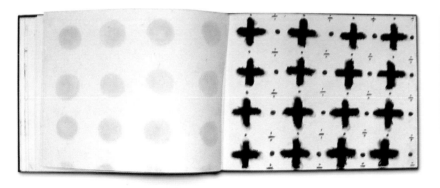

Lotte Rømer
Musician, Composer and Author
Copenhagen

Lotte was born in 1950. Over the past 25 years, she has released many albums in her own name and collaborated with many other artists, both as a singer, musician and composer. Since 1970, she has given over two thousand live performances throughout Europe. Lotte has also appeared on numerous TV programmes, as a soloist, musician and host. In 1997, she made her debut as an author with her memoirs *The Wings of the Silver Bird* following it up in 1998 with an extensive lecture series based on her experiences living with impaired hearing. In November 1999, Lotte published her second book *What?* which she subsequently developed into a film with the same name. Since 1992, she has written articles, essays and interviews in several newspapers and magazines.

Inspiration
Lots of different things inspire me. They can be very visual things like light, darkness, reflections on the wall or contrasts. Or they can be movement, physical activity, going for a ride on my bike, travelling, skiing or driving. If I'm stuck, I go away for a few days. I find a café where I can sit and watch people. I'm inspired by the scenarios and stories that take place around me.

I always try to seek inspiration in new places and objects.

I love humour. There's nothing as healing as a really good laugh. Good company is also very inspiring.

I collect art, paintings, pictures, photographs, fabric, textiles, stones, CDs, stories, swimsuits and lots of sunglasses.

Working environment
I get my best ideas in my car. In a car you can't do anything practical, so your thoughts start wandering off into a different mode. It's like a small world which no one else can enter. There's something about speed. I become one with the engine, while nature flies by. It's as if working on two levels; I'm driving and at the same time I am somewhere else. Working out how to solve a problem always happens in my car.

Working process
I start by cleaning up. It gives me peace and helps me clear my thoughts. For years I felt bad about it. I used to wonder "why do I always have to move the bookshelves before I can get started?" But now I know I need the

time to focus, collect my thoughts and sharpen my thinking. It isn't just a waste of time.

When I'm composing I can sit and listen to the sound of my grand piano and let that inspire me. At other times it might be a voice, a picture or an experience that triggers me, and I start to hear things.

What happens in my mind then happens very quickly. An opera that takes two hours to perform can be formed within five minutes. It's just like a sculptor who can suddenly see the whole piece before he starts.

The fact that I'm hard of hearing sometimes gives me a new approach. I think I hear one thing, but in reality I hear something else. I make positive connections and, as a result, create new things. Once I found inspiration in what I thought was an African choir performing in the street, but when I actually went down to the street I realised the noise was coming from a concrete mixer.

Motivation
The ability to make a difference motivates me. I also find it very motivating to meet new people.

At the moment, I need another two days a week for all the things I would like to do.

Reading
I don't read as much as I would like. I love good books. Maybe a thriller for relaxation, or a book about personal development or spirituality.

Most inspiring person
Sting. His voice and his music.

"I get my best ideas in my car"

"I always try to seek
inspiration in new
places and things"

Thomas Sandell

Architect, Interior Architect,
Sandell Sandberg
Stockholm

Thomas Sandell was born in 1959.
He graduated with a master's
degree in architecture and engi-
neering from the Royal Institute
of Technology in 1985. In 1995,
he founded the multi-disciplinary
design group, Sandell Sandberg,
which combines architecture,
design and advertising. Thomas
has designed several acclaimed
interiors, including Stockholm's
Museum of Modern Art and
Swedish Museum of Architecture.
As a furniture designer, Thomas has
collaborated with many renowned
furniture producers, such as Artek,
Asplund, B&B Italia, Cappellini,
CBI, Gärsnäs, IKEA, Källemo,
Mobileffe, R.O.O.M., Rydéns,
Tibrokök and Tronconi. He has
received countless design awards
and until 2002 he was president
of SAR, the National Association
of Swedish Architects.

Inspiration

I find childhood a huge source of inspiration. A sort of
memory bank. It lays the foundation for what you do
later in life.

Travelling often stimulates me. When you travel,
you suddenly find yourself open to impressions in a
completely different way. You can sit on a terrace in Italy
and stare at a saltcellar and think it looks absolutely
fantastic. Then, when you're back home you realise
that they have exactly the same saltcellar in your local
restaurant, but you just hadn't noticed it there.
Aside from that, I collect art.

Working environment

My workplace is open-plan and messy. That's how I
work best.

Working process

When I get a new assignment, I usually have an idea of
what I want to do straight away. Then I try to steer the
project so that the solution ends up as close as possible
to that first idea.
Sometimes even when you realise you're on a dead-end
street, you still hold on to that original idea, but then
you just have to let it go and start all over again. By
then, though, you'll have learned from your mistakes
and will know all the problems, so coming up with a
new solution will be much quicker.

If you get stuck, you just have to keep going. Sooner or
later it will happen. Or you have to start all over again.

I can think virtually anywhere. I usually get good ideas
in the summer when I'm on the ferryboat on my way to
work. Or in the evenings when I relax in front of the TV,
the pieces often fall into place, and that's when I usually
get my best ideas. For me the office usually represents
just an administrative period in the middle of the day.
If I have trouble getting into the right frame of mind,
I leave the office or take time off.

Motivation

Like so many other designers, I'm motivated by vanity.
I like publicity, praise and appreciation. And that people
like and use my things.

Reading

I read all sorts of stuff. Biographies, documentaries,
classical novels and magazines.

Most inspiring person

Alvar Aalto.

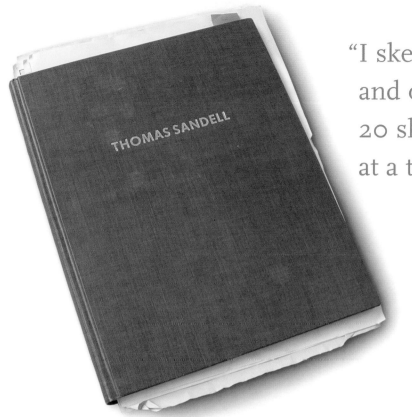

"I sketch a lot,
and order
20 sketchbooks
at a time"

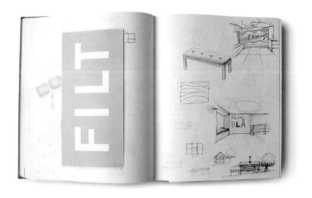

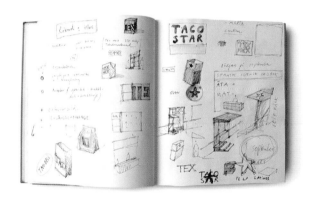

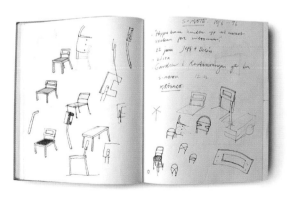

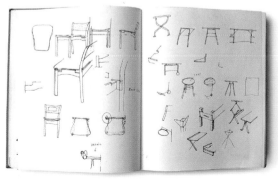

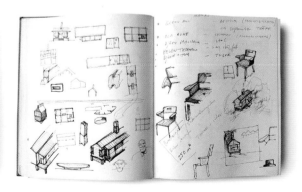

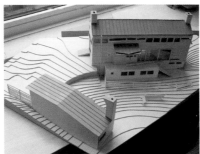

"My office is open-plan and messy. That's how I work the best"

Andrew Smart
Art Director,
Robert/Boisen and Likeminded
Copenhagen

Andrew was born in Durham in 1969. After working as an illustrator in his native Northeast England, Andrew won a scholarship at the School of Communication Arts in London. It was here he teamed up with Roger Beckett and was hired by London advertising agency Bartle Bogle Hegarty. The partnership went on to create distinctive work for such clients as Levi's, Audi, Lego, Lynx and Nike, and reaped awards from Cannes, British Television Advertising, Eurobest, Campaign Print and Posters. Andrew left BBH as creative director and followed his wife to her native Denmark. He continued his success as creative director at DDB in Copenhagen, winning gold at Eurobest for his work with the Østre Gasværk Teater. In 2003, Andrew joined local agency of the year Robert/Boisen and Likeminded.

Inspiration

I find it hard to identify specific sources of inspiration because they're so random for me. However, generally speaking, combinations of seemingly opposing forces seem to get me thinking creatively. Loud music in a tranquil setting or something very high-tech combined with something very low-tech. Slapstick comedy combined with elegance. I know it sounds a little abstract, but I can't point at specific objects, experiences or events. It's more complex than that. It's kind of a feeling or mood I find myself in. I wish I was better at recognising or recreating these seemingly random triggers. It would make life a lot simpler. I think it's about trying to notice everything.

Working environment

Variation works for me. I find it almost essential to vary my surroundings if I want ideas to come, especially if I'm stuck. I prefer new places or situations. All I need is a way of recording my thoughts. A pen and paper or my PowerBook. I don't like too much noise or distraction around me. I hate background music. Over the years I have tried collecting things because I suppose I thought I ought to. You know the kind of stuff. Japanese plastic toys. Old football annuals. It never helped me, so I stopped. Looking back, I think it was pretentious.

Working process

I start every project by collecting my instinctive thoughts. I allow myself to be naive and idealistic. I use these first-round thoughts as a kind of sanity check later in the process. It's my 'normal person's' view of the problem before my vision becomes clouded by the process. The second phase is about researching and collecting information. Later, I often try and sneak up on a problem. I consciously try and put it out of my mind and then come back to it suddenly. I try to bump-start ideas. I think what I'm trying to do is manufacture the instinctive phase again, having now loaded up with information. And when it all gets too much, there's nothing like a long bike ride.

Reading

I don't read enough, which I feel really bad about. I scan. I'm a very lazy reader. Having a family has also forced me to prioritise what I read and watch. I love the internet. I find the blogosphere very inspiring. *The Guardian, Howies catalogues, Wired, Viz,* and anything to do with cycling.

Motivation

I think we need to re-think the way we do business. Capitalism in its current predatory form clearly isn't working that well. I am interested in the Authentic Business movement, sustainable capitalism and more positive and respectful ways for business to contribute to the future. I urge anyone who works in a marketing-related industry to read Mark Barden's speech to the APG Conference in 2002, which you can find at: www.authenticbusiness.co.uk/archive/changeamerica/

Most inspiring person

Comedian: Bill Hicks. Artist: Bill Drummond.
Author: Neil Crofts and Mark Barden for his speech.

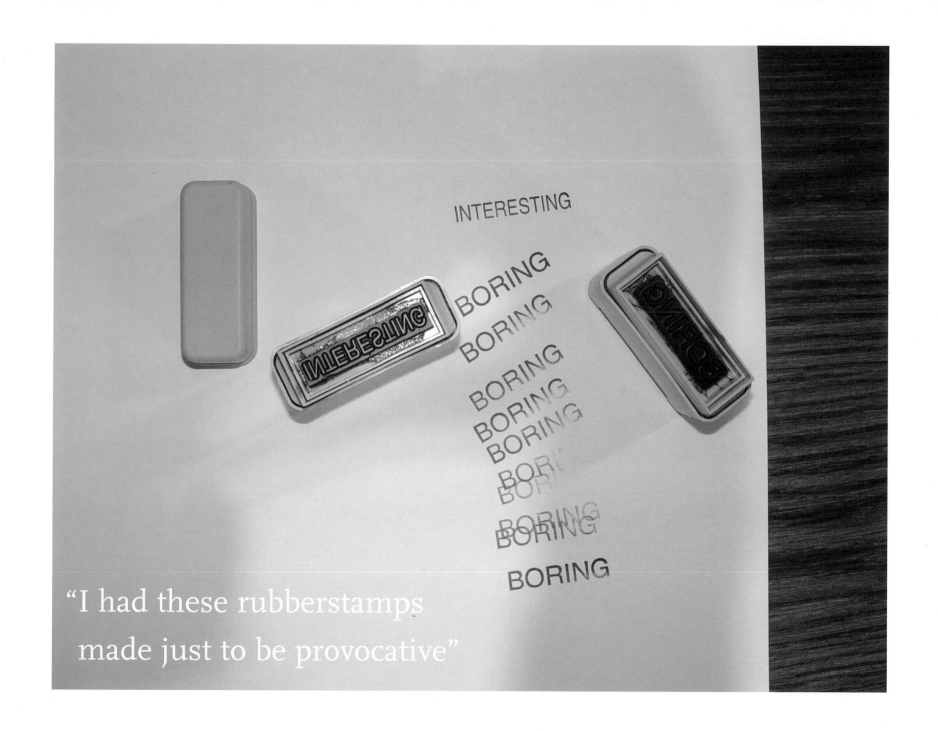

INTERESTING

BORING
BORING

BORING
BORING
BORING

BOR
BOR

BORING
BORING

BORING

"I had these rubberstamps
made just to be provocative"

"If you can't find the right answer, look for the right question"

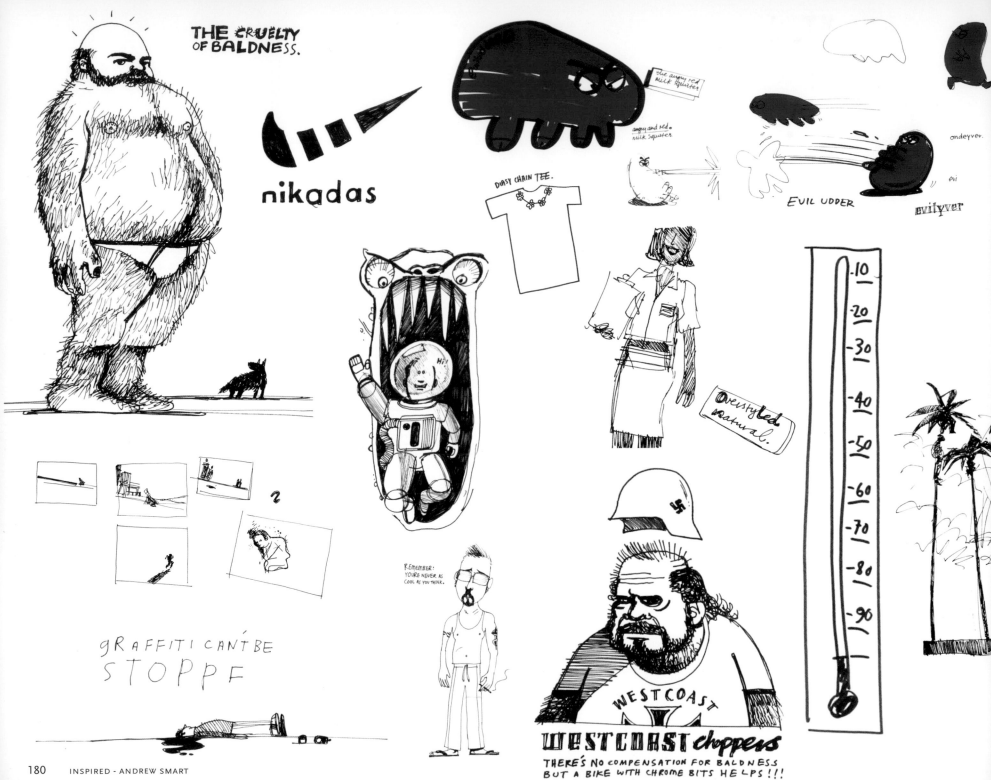

THE CRUELTY OF BALDNESS.

nikadas

the angry red milk squirter

angry and red milk squirter

DIASY CHAIN TEE.

EVIL UDDER

ondeyver.
evil
evilyver

Overstyled natural.

-10
-20
-30
-40
-50
-60
-70
-80
-90

Hi!

REMEMBER:
YOU'RE NEVER AS
COOL AS YOU THINK.

gRAFFITI CAN'T BE STOPPF

WEST COAST

WESTCOAST choppers
THERE'S NO COMPENSATION FOR BALDNESS
BUT A BIKE WITH CHROME BITS HELPS!!!

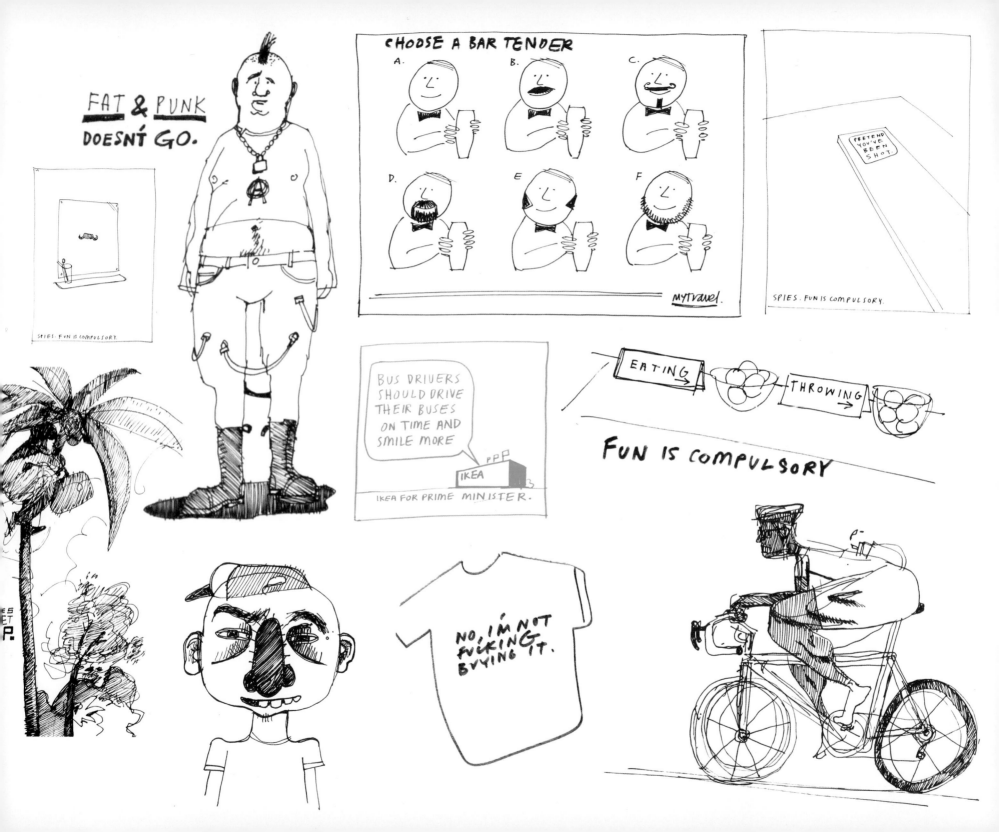

Idea

"A change of environment always work for me"

Paul Smith

Designer, Chairman and Founder,
Paul Smith Limited
London

Paul opened his first boutique in a tiny shop in his hometown of Nottingham, England in 1970. While still attending evening classes in tailoring and with encouragement from his girlfriend Pauline Denyer, now his wife, he continued to develop his business. In 1976, Paul showed his first menswear collection in Paris. Within 20 years of entering the fashion world, he had established himself as the pre-eminent British designer. Today Paul Smith is global. There are 13 different collections in total and the Paul Smith brand is wholesaled to 55 countries worldwide. Paul is still an integral part of the company, both as designer and chairman. He is involved with every aspect of the business and as a result, Paul Smith Limited retains a personal touch often missing from companies of a similar size.

Inspiration

Inspiration comes from observation. When I'm travelling, it can be a local way of dressing, an army or a postal uniform, or how people put colours together. I get inspiration from seeing things that are out of context. It could be a Ferrari parked outside a 14th-century monastery. The fact that they clash with each other could be the inspiration for combining a denim shirt with a cashmere suit, or putting a modern chair in a traditional environment.

I never really take any notice of other designers. As a designer, I think you should be bright enough to be able to create original ideas from an empty sheet of paper, rather than copying from something that already exists.

Working environment

My wife is an artist and most of our friends are not in fashion. They are either in art, photography, architecture or graphic design. So most of the time I'm surrounded by all of those things. I collect large quantities of the same things. But I can't really call it collecting in a true sense, because I always think of a collector as someone who has knowledge about what they collect.

Working process

I never approach a job as such. It's always there. It just flows along like a river. I never have a dedicated day or hour for a specific job, unless I'm working with my assistants. If, for instance, we are working on a new collection, we might go away to a hotel in the countryside. But I will have started working on the collection, and will already have a pile of ideas. I've always got a little notebook in my jacket, a scrap of paper or the back of

an envelope with something written on it. I use a notebook and pencil every day of my life and I always carry a camera, which I use as a visual diary. I can't draw very well, so I mostly design in words. I might write 'zips' on a piece of paper or 'zips in unusual places', 'too many zips', 'brightly coloured zips', 'long and short zips' and that will be enough for me.

I look at things, and ideas immediately develop in my head. I can look at something completely unrelated to fashion, say some vegetables for example, and they suddenly become a shirt pattern. I never think of ideas, they just come to me. It's easy. In fact I have too many ideas. I'm very inquisitive and curious about things. But I try to not to let my mind get too cluttered with information. I never watch television or use the internet for example. I like to think I'm a free spirit and lateral thinker. Hopefully I have a very childlike view of the world. Childlike, not childish. A friend of mine once said: "You walk down the road and see fifty things, and I walk down the same road and see only three things."

I think you can train yourself to observe more, and to act on your observations.

Reading

It has to be something that I'm interested in, rather than just a book. I like books about real life.

Motivation

My love of life. And the fact that life is too short.

Inspiring person

My wife Pauline. She has inspired me the most and always kept my feet on the ground.

"I use a notebook
and pencil every day"

"The office above the shop
is representative of my head"

RECEPTION WALL IN THE PAUL SMITH OFFICE
IN COVENT GARDEN, LONDON.

PAUL SMITH'S OWN BOOK 'YOU CAN
FIND INSPIRATION IN EVERYTHING'.

Garech & Declan Stone

Graphic Designers,
Founders of The Stone Twins
Amsterdam

Declan and Garech Stone were born
in 1970 in Dublin, Ireland. Both
received B.A. Hons degrees in visual
communication from the National
College of Art + Design, Dublin.
Garech then freelanced in London
before becoming a senior designer
at Vorm Vijf, The Hague. Declan
freelanced in Dublin, and then
joined Samenwerkende Ontwerpers
in Amsterdam, as senior designer.
In 1999, they founded The Stone
Twins, a creative communications
agency specialising in highly
creative, witty and strategic brand
creation for some of the Netherlands'
biggest companies, including IKEA
Nederland, ING Bank, Sony Ericsson,
Usual Suspects, Virgin Records
Benelux and ELLE. The company has
won many awards and Declan and
Garech's recent book Logo R.I.P. has
won international acclaim. Both are
regular guest-lecturers at the Willem
de Koning Academie, Rotterdam,
and the National College of Art &
Design, Dublin (NCAD).

Inspiration

Inspiration is everywhere. We get it from reading,
watching TV, going to the cinema, hanging in bars or by
meeting interesting people. We find it in the extremities
of hi and lo culture: in an art gallery or the terraces at a
football game. We're avid collectors of stuff, whether it's
posters, antique books, bruises, knickknacks or Catholic
paraphernalia.

Working environment

We don't feel inhibited by not having an actual studio
space. Modern technology means we are accessible
at any time as well as offering different locations for
meeting clients, brainstorming or checking proofs. In
fact, this concept is quite liberating and offers unlimited
cubic head-space. Six years on, it seems to work well
for us...

Working process

Our initial approach to an assignment is to ask and
probe. We then perform extensive research – which
could mean delving into the environment of the client,
a chat with the target audience, a look at competitors,
a Google-search or going to a library. We always have
our notebooks with us for sketching or making notes.
To get into the right frame of mind, we change our
environment. We go for a walk, or drink nice coffee in
a cheesy snackbar. At the beginning of a project,
we often work separately and then meet up to cross-
fertilise, improve or abuse each other's approach. After
preliminary pencil sketches – where we can resolve an
idea – tasks are delegated. Only then, do we begin to
implement the concepts on a computer. In most of our
projects, apart from trying to answer the client's brief
and making a striking visual aesthetic, we aim for a
solution that is witty, engaging and memorable.

Motivation

We feel privileged to be doing what we do. We love
meeting new people and absorbing ourselves in different subject matters. It's very stimulating to juggle the
diverse concerns and needs of financial institutions,
cultural organisations or advertising agencies – which
we often perform on a daily basis. I suppose we enjoy
the schizophrenic nature of our profession.

Reading

We read a lot of diverse things – we're both obsessive
about current affairs, history, trade/commerce and, of
course, design journals. Recently, Garech is stimulated
by the books of Thomas L Friedman, whilst Declan is
reading about the Roman Empire.

Most inspiring person

Each other... ha, ha. Where do we start? Roy Keane,
Richard Branson, Norman Foster, Alan Fletcher, Trevor
Horn, Anton Corbijn, Ricky Gervais, Damien Hirst and
our granny.

"The icons of the church have always inspired us"

Carouschka Streijffert

Interior Architect,
Set Designer and Artist
Stockholm

Born in 1955 in Stockholm,
Carouschka studied classic art,
furniture and interior design at the
University College of Arts, Crafts and
Design in Stockholm. After graduating, she started her career working
at various architectural firms before
eventually setting up her own company, Carouschka AB in 1978. Over
the years, Carouschka's career has
diversified, bringing her success as
an author, scriptwriter, set designer
and exhibition designer. Her own
work has been exhibited on numerous occasions and her design work
has been commissioned by such
clients as Pukeberg. Carouschka is
also committed to education, and
works as a lecturer and moderator
for several art schools in Sweden.

Inspiration

I'm inspired by 'urban rubbish'. I like recycling material that other people haven't even seen yet. Right now
I'm in a period of transition. I'm switching from urban
materials, such as tickets, to more natural materials
like sticks.

When I work as an interior architect and set designer,
I'm very functionalistic, but with a certain playfulness.
Early on in my career, I learned how to work with three-
dimensional aspects, volume, construction and material.
This has since helped me to do many other things.

When I travel, I always find a lot of material for my
collages. I also like going to museums, but I always
rush through very quickly. For me it's a way of checking
what's happening, as well as a way of measuring myself.

Working environment

I always have a lot of inspirational material around
me. A collection of tickets for example. Bowls – there's
something really feminine about them, like wombs.
I've also got tons of boxes full of bits of paper.

Working process

When I start, I find a big empty white sheet of paper
wonderful. I quickly become part of my projects, like a
small ant stepping into a problem. My body, brain and
senses are all inside the rooms I'm creating.
I can use my imagination so vividly that I walk around in
my own sketches, and meet other people there as well.
It's almost like a kind of meditation. I close off everything else and live in the project.

When creativity kicks in, a large amount of resistance
inevitably also comes with it. You start doubting and ask
"is this good?", "is this right?" This period of resistance
happens in all creative processes. The challenge is to
work through it and I have always been very good at
that. During this period, you reconsider thoughts and
ideas and improve them. It's hard work and you have to
be a fighter.

Quietness and concentration are important when
creating the right mood, as is the pressure of a deadline.
I never get stuck. I always work really hard and I prefer
projects to be complex.

Motivation

As a little child I was often misunderstood, and I guess
I'm still busy trying to be understood.
I also have this enormous need to communicate. So I
talk through my sketches.

Reading

I read psychology books and *Domus* magazine.

Most inspiring person

Kurt Schwitters and Le Corbusier.

"I don't work with a computer. For me, a computer is a limitation. It can't possibly keep up with what goes on in my head"

"Urban rubbish inspires me"

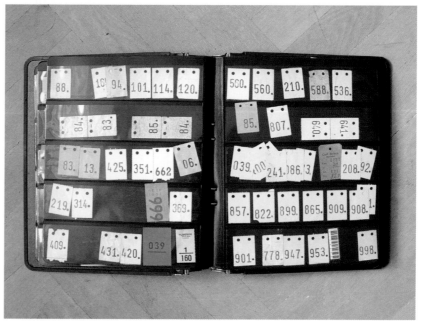

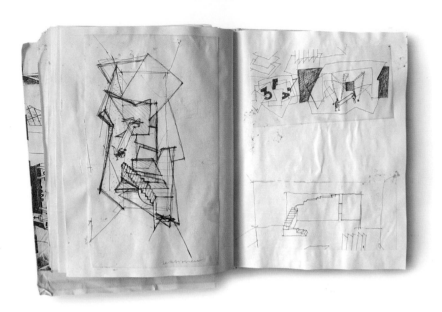

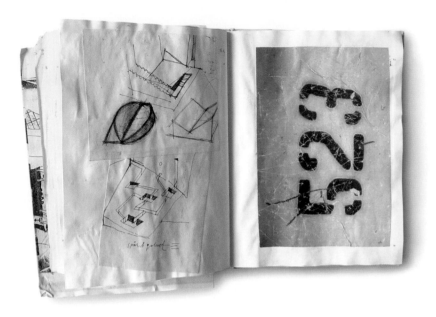

"Sketching is the most important part of a project"

"I make collages out of nature"

"When creativity kicks in, a large amount of resistance inevitably also comes with it"

CAROUSCHKA'S COMBINED HOME
AND STUDIO IN STOCKHOLM.

Rob Wagemans
Founder of Concrete Architects
Amsterdam

Rob was born in Eindhoven in
1973 and studied architecture in
Utrecht. He set up in business
as an independent designer,
earning numerous commissions
while continuing his education
at Amsterdam's University of
Construction, where he earned a
masters degree. In 1997, Rob started
Concrete Architects together with
Gilian Schrofer and Erik van Dillen.
Erik van Dillen left the company in
2000 and Gilian in 2004, leaving
Rob as a director and sole owner
of the company. Throughout his
career, Rob has worked on many
commercial interior design assignments and prestigious projects with
Concrete, and continues to win a
variety of awards along the way.

Inspiration
My sources of inspiration are very wide-ranging and
constantly changing... art, society, music and fashion.
I try to look for inspiration were you wouldn't necessarily
expect to find it. If I have a brief for a film, I don't go
and look at other films, but at public transport or art. If
I have an assignment for a museum, I might go to IKEA
for inspiration. In the end, frustration is my greatest
source of inspiration.

Working environment
I try to surround myself with happiness. Good food,
good drinks. The city, Amsterdam, is important to
me. People working, living and going out on the same
square metre. My life is all about my hobby, because it's
my work.
I also collect some furniture and art.

Working process
I get into the right frame of mind by having fun and
creating a relaxed atmosphere. I start by checking the
boundaries, then I fight those constraints. I simplify the
brief and try to find and remove the dogmas. I make
sketches in my head, draw and make models.

Tuesdays between 4 and 7 p.m. I always set aside for
creative time. Then we go for dinner and talk. The rest of
the week is just business.

I try to get rid of fear. Fear is my biggest opponent.
I don't want to deal with clients who are scared of losing
their jobs, but prefer entrepreneurs willing to take risks.
You can't create anything new if you are scared or afraid
of innovation.
If I'm getting nowhere, I stop and try something else,
but I never really get stuck. I might even give the assignment back if I can't solve the client's problem to my
satisfaction. But I have to say that nine times out of ten
the client is surprised by our solution.

Motivation
I can make a lot happen. I can make the world a bit
better through good architecture.

Reading
Ten magazines a week. But I'm dyslexic, so...

Most inspiring person
Lars von Trier and Peter Greenaway.

"Frustration is my
greatest source
of inspiration"

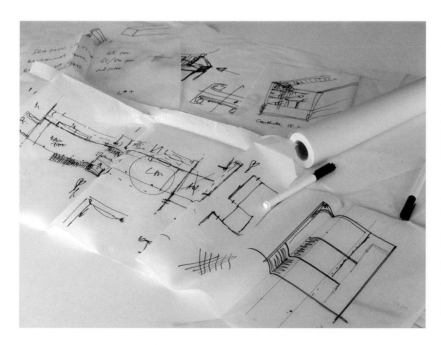

"Fear is my biggest opponent. I don't want to deal with clients who are scared of losing their jobs, but prefer entrepreneurs willing to take risks"

CONCRETE'S STUDIO IN
THE HEART OF AMSTERDAM.

Stina Wirsén

Illustrator
Stockholm

Stina Wirsén was educated at Nyckelviksskolan and Konstfack in Stockholm. She graduated with a master's degree in graphic design and illustration in 1992. While studying, she started a long-term collaboration with the Swedish national newspaper *Dagens Nyheter,* which resulted in her becoming head of illustration in 1997. Stina has received awards from The Society of Newspaper Design and The Society of Scandinavian Illustrators and has also won the prestigious Elsa Beskow Award for children's book illustrations. She has worked with magazines such as *Food & Wine, Dwell* and *Seventeen,* and such clients as IKEA, Telia, Nordtedts, Bonniers, Ytterborn & Fuentes and Brindfors.

Inspiration

I follow trends and movements in society. I'm fascinated by fashion, as it's really about ideas and reflects what's happening in society.
I also get inspiration from my children. They're always drawing.
Listening in on people on the bus and on the underground is also very inspiring. I look at things everywhere, from flea markets to exhibitions.

Working environment

What I surround myself with depends on what I'm working with. After each project I do a big clean-up.

Working process

I suck up as much information as I can and then make sure that I have time by myself. I create a sort of free zone.

I get my best ideas through discussions. I always try to get to the essence of a brief through a lot of discussion. I do a lot of research, talk to journalists, sketch and doodle, and all of a sudden something just happens. If I get stuck, it's usually because there's something wrong with the basic idea, then I have to go back and have a re-think. Sometimes it helps to work on something else for a while.

Motivation

I think what I do is both important and fun.

Reading

I have no favourite magazines.

Most inspiring person

The Swedish writer Barbro Lindgren. The texts of her books are fantastic. Especially the early ones: *Loranga, Världshemligt* and *Bladen brinner.* They're like self-portraits. She describes her own childhood in a lovely and unpretentious way. She also did all the illustrations herself.

"I get inspiration
from my children"

"I suck up as much information as I can, and then make sure that I have time on my own, I create a sort of free zone"

Acknowledgements

First of all, we would like to thank all the people featured in this book for their time and for sharing their work, thoughts and secrets with us. We would also like to give special thanks to the following people without whose help, patience and endurance we couldn't have made this book: Frank Boon, Helen Dyrbye, John Farr, Peter Gravesen, Lillian Nielsen, Helle Barth, Jørgen Vester, Rietje van Vreden, Kate Nielsen, and last but not least Ron and Andrew.

About the authors

Kiki Hartmann was born in Sweden, and studied at the RMI-Berghs School of Communication in Stockholm and subsequently at the School of Communication Arts in London. Her design career spans nearly twenty years, during which she has been based in Stockholm, London and most recently in Amsterdam, where she currently works as design director at VBAT. Her work has been recognised and awarded at the New York Festivals, Mercury Awards and D&AD amongst others. Kiki has guest-lectured at The Graphic Arts Institute of Denmark and Berghs School of Communication in Stockholm. She also has a great passion for photography and her work has been exhibited at various galleries in the Netherlands.

Born in Denmark, Dorte Nielsen studied at The Graphic Arts Institute of Denmark and later at the School of Communication Arts in London. For most of the 90's she worked as an art director in London. Her advertising work there, won her recognition at the Cannes International Advertising Festival, D&AD, the British Television Awards, Epica, London International Advertising awards, the Campaign Poster Awards amongst others. Since moving back to Denmark, Dorte has been lecturing in creativity and creative thinking at The Graphic Arts Institute of Denmark. She is also the author of *Idébogen, (Grafisk Litteratur 2001),* and several articles on creative thinking.